Ma

Amish White Christmas

Christmas

THREE Complete Novellas

Snowflakes on Goose Pond

Snow Angels

The Gingerbread Haus

Samantha Jillian Bayarr

All scripture references in this book used from New International Version of the Bible

Be informed about all contests and book giveaways by following me on Facebook:
http://www.facebook.com/SamanthaBayarr

CHAT with me on my Facebook Group,
Amish Friendship Bread

Also by Samantha Jillian Bayarr

Jacob's Daughter Amish Collection
Jacob's Daughter
Amish Winter Wonderland
Under the Mulberry Tree
Amish Winter of Promises
Chasing Fireflies
Amish Summer of Courage
Under the Harvest Moon

Amish Romance
The Quilter's Son
An Amish Christmas Wish
Amish White Christmas
Amish Love Letters
The Amish Gardener

Amish Love Series
An Amish Harvest
An Amish Courtship
An Amish Widower
Amish Sisters

LWF Amish Series
Little Wild Flower Book I
Little Wild Flower Book II
The Taming of a Wild Flower
Little Wild Flower in Bloom
Little Wild Flower's Journey

Christian Romance
Milk Maid in Heaven
The Anniversary

Christian Historical Romance
A Sheriff's Legacy: Book One
Preacher Outlaw: Book Two
Cattle Rustler in Petticoats: Book Three

**Please note: All editions may not be available yet.
Please check online for availability.**

Snowflakes on Goose Pond

A Novella

Chapter One

"Ruby, stop showing off," Priscilla reprimanded her cousin. "It isn't going to make Jesse Fisher notice you."

Priscilla, or *Prissy,* as Ruby had always called her overbearing cousin, could be rude and downright embarrassing at times. Prissy had suddenly become very bossy toward her, constantly reminding Ruby that she was a few months older. Ruby had wished more than once that her cousin had never come to live in the same community. At first she had been excited, having not seen Prissy for more than a year, but now that they had been baptized, Prissy had turned competitive, vying for the attention of all the eligible *menner* in their youth group—especially Jesse Fisher.

"I'm not showing off, Prissy. I can't help it that I'm a *gut* skater. It's taken years of practice to skate this well."

Priscilla narrowed her eyes at Ruby. "I don't like the way Jesse is looking at you."

"I don't even like him," Ruby said in her defense. "You can have him. You two seem to have a lot in common. You're both rude."

She hadn't meant to be so harsh, but Prissy was becoming so irritating she could barely stand to be around her anymore. She especially hadn't meant to call Jesse rude, because truthfully, she liked him, but was afraid to admit it.

Priscilla pursed her lips "Well, you're no picnic either Ruby—you're boring!" She skated toward Jesse's group, leaving Ruby feeling guilty for her harsh words.

Ruby had always thought of Jesse Fisher as *unreachable.* Though he was two years older than Ruby, she had been aware of his popularity from the time they were in school. Even now, Jesse was the center of all the attention from all the women in the youth group—especially from Priscilla. He was the most handsome, and everyone liked him—even Ruby, who found him to be almost as overbearing as Prissy sometimes.

Ruby skated further away from her cousin, trying to enjoy the snowflakes that gathered on the thick surface of the frozen pond. She was aware that

Jesse watched her, but she didn't understand why. She loved to skate more than anything, and had even learned to inline skate over the summer when she'd finally saved up enough money to purchase a pair of the popular skates. At nearly twenty-three, her *bruder,* Gabriel, had teased her and told her she was too old for such a thing, but skating made her happy. With no offers for buggy rides from any of the *menner* in the youth group, she needed something to occupy her free time.

It wasn't that Ruby was trying to make herself unavailable for dates; she simply wasn't being asked. She assumed it was because she wasn't as talkative as Priscilla, but sometimes, Ruby thought Priscilla talked too much. Her cousin had made a point to be the center of attention ever since she'd come to live in the community, and Prissy sure did let everyone know she was there. Gabriel had referred to their cousin as a *squeaky wheel,* and Ruby agreed.

Gliding happily across to the other side of the large pond, Ruby felt free from the watchful eyes of Prissy and Jesse. Being younger than Prissy, Ruby could only guess that Jesse and his friends watched her looking for a reason to tease her. Jesse's friends were often overheard teasing others in the youth group, and Ruby believed they acted that way because they were immature and insecure. She'd never seen or heard anything of the sort from Jesse himself, but the crowd he kept did not do well for his reputation in Ruby's opinion. None of them ever skated; they stood at the edge of the pond and made jokes whenever someone would slip on the ice. It angered Ruby that they showed up only for the opportunity to tease others.

The sun began to sink over the horizon, but Ruby continued to skate away from the others. She formed a *figure-eight* as she skimmed the ice effortlessly. When she skated, she felt free from the pressure of responsibilities to care for her *daed* and *bruder*—free from Prissy's ridicule. The blades of her skates scraped the ice as she stopped suddenly, spraying a wave of ice and snow toward an onlooker—Jesse Fisher.

Thinking she had been alone, Ruby wondered how Jesse had managed to walk the perimeter of the pond without her noticing. But suddenly, he was standing at the edge watching her as though she was performing just for him. Feeling embarrassed, she non-conspicuously looked around to see if anyone had followed him to the far edge of the pond. He stood there alone, and even Prissy was nowhere in sight. Why had he followed her, and why was he so interested in watching her?

It made her nervous.

Trying her best to ignore Jesse's presence at the edge of the pond, Ruby skated and twirled her most favorite moves across the ice. Was she showing off for Jesse? Perhaps just a little, but it made her feel important that he should choose to watch her so closely. Was it possible that he was about to ask her for a sleigh ride? She had walked to the skating party with Prissy, and it was beginning to get dark—perfect for a romantic sleigh ride with Jesse.

Chapter Two

"I'd love a ride home, Jesse," Prissy said, flirtation dripping from her tongue.

Where had Prissy come from? Hadn't Jesse just asked *Ruby* if he could give her a ride home? They were the only two people at the far end of the pond—weren't they? But there was Prissy, accepting an invitation and intruding on Ruby's one chance to get a sleigh ride from the most handsome *mann* in the youth group.

Jesse cleared his throat. "I would be happy to take you *both* home," he offered.

Ruby fumed.

He had asked *her*—hadn't he? But before she could give her answer, Prissy had pushed her way into Ruby's one chance at finding out why Jesse would ask her in the first place. Or had she imagined he'd asked *her*—only because that is what she hoped for deep down somewhere in her subconscious?

Priscilla's farm was further from the pond than Ruby's, which meant the two of them would ride alone for nearly half a mile after dropping her off. That was plenty of time for Prissy to talk ill of Ruby behind her back. It saddened her to think that her cousin was capable of such a thing, but she wouldn't be surprised if Prissy did exactly that.

Jesse helped them into his sleigh one-by-one, Priscilla lingering over the hand he offered in assistance. Ruby had never been that close to Jesse, and his deep blue eyes paralyzed her for a moment, holding her captive in the kindness she'd never seen in them. She wasn't prepared to see kindness in his eyes, and it erased every ill thought she'd ever had about him. Was it possible he was not like his friends? They were crude at times, but up-close, Jesse didn't fit that description at all.

Ruby settled in on the end of the bench seat of the sleigh while Jesse sat on the other side of Priscilla. A low giggle erupted from her cousin as Jesse settled in beside her. Could she be any more obvious? Ruby tried not to let Prissy bother her as she forced herself to enjoy her first sleigh ride with a *mann*—even if she wasn't alone with him.

I can dream, can't I? If I look up into the sky and watch the snowflakes blending with the stars, I can pretend we are alone on such a romantic night as this…

"Ruby, get out of the sleigh," Prissy was shouting at her.

Embarrassed, Ruby hadn't realized they had stopped in front of her *haus,* and was grateful it was too dark for Jesse to see her inflamed cheeks. How had they gotten to her farm so quickly? She jumped down from the sleigh before Jesse had the chance to assist her.

"Will I see you at the pond tomorrow?" Jesse asked in his smoky baritone.

His question surprised Ruby, but the look in his eyes was hopeful. Confused, Ruby merely nodded.

"Can we go?" Prissy called from the sleigh. "I'm cold."

Prissy's whining broke the spell between Ruby and Jesse, and he excused himself abruptly. Ruby watched as he climbed back up next to Prissy and grabbed the reins. She hadn't moved from the center of the bench even though Ruby was no longer next to her. Tipping her head over her shoulder, Prissy flashed Ruby a crooked smile of satisfaction before Jesse's sleigh took off. Ruby's heart sank as she watched them disappear into the snowy night.

✳✳✳✳

"I wouldn't be surprised if we were engaged by Christmas," Prissy boasted with a prideful tone.

Ruby tried her best to ignore her cousin as they walked to Goose Pond. If what Prissy was saying was true, then Ruby didn't stand a chance with Jesse, and she had imagined the brief connection between them last night. It was probably for the best. Perhaps having a beau would calm Prissy and keep her out of Ruby's hair. Even if Ruby had taken a sudden interest in Jesse, it didn't mean she would be the one to win his heart. Not if Prissy had anything to do with it. As competitive as Prissy was, she would make certain that Ruby had no chance with Jesse if it was up to her.

Stepping onto the ice, Ruby skated away from Prissy and the gathering crowd of youth. She wanted to be alone—free to skate—the only thing that made her happy. She needed to clear her head of thoughts of hope where Jesse was concerned. She would never begrudge her cousin the chance at happiness, and that meant she had to let go of all romantic thoughts of Jesse. It seemed that *Gott* had other plans for her life, and it just didn't include Jesse—no matter how much *she* might have wanted it to.

Snow falling at her feet made skating a bit more challenging, but Jesse's friends would be along soon with brooms to clear the ice. Ruby didn't mind the snow as she twirled, her face aimed at the sky. Cold snowflakes touched her cheeks as she closed her eyes and twirled, oblivious of her surroundings. She was one with the ice, in her own world with the snow that drifted thick from the gray sky above.

"You make it look so easy."

Jesse's smoky voice startled her, nearly causing her to fall. How had he gotten so close to her again without her being aware of his presence?

Ruby didn't look him in the eye for fear he would hypnotize her again with his charm. "I've been skating since I could walk."

"You've improved over the years. It seems every year I see a new move that astonishes me. That spin you just did is a new one."

Ruby stopped and stared at him, surprised once again by his statements. He had noticed her over the years enough to know her skating had improved? Was this some kind of joke?

Jesse pushed the broom sheepishly, clearing the snow in her path. "I was hoping you would consider teaching me to skate."

Chapter Three

Ruby nearly lost her footing on the ice with Jesse so near. Had he just asked her to teach him how to skate?

Jesse waved the broom in front of her. "Did you hear me, Ruby?"

He knows my name! He's been watching me skate all these years! Is it possible he likes me?

"I'd like to skate at the Christmas party, but I don't know how. Will you teach me? I'm willing to pay you for the lessons," he offered.

There it was. The Christmas Skate consisted generally of couples, and hopefuls. Since he'd offered to pay her and hadn't invited her to the Skate, she could only believe he intended to ask Prissy. All he wanted from *her* was skating lessons so he could ask her cousin to the Christmas Skate. Prissy had talked the whole morning about the romantic connection they'd made when he'd taken her home last night.

Ruby sank her teeth into her bottom lip to squelch the tears that pooled behind her eyes and agreed to be his coach. She would do it for her cousin's sake, even though Prissy did not deserve Ruby's kindness.

"Do you have skates?"

"*Nee,* but I can get some later this afternoon and have them for tomorrow," Jesse said eagerly.

"No need to pay me," Ruby said, trying not to grit her teeth. "You can learn without skates for now. Your first lesson will be easier without the skates. I can begin with teaching you the basics about how to glide across the ice."

Jesse stood close to Ruby, his nearness stealing away her every thought. How was she going to manage teaching him to skate if he was going to stand this close to her the entire time? His blue eyes sparkled at her, capturing her gaze in his. She tried to look away, but she was frozen like an icicle, unable to move. The curve of his smile was gentle and inviting, pulling her deeper into her romantic thoughts she had tried to rid herself of only a few moments before.

Ruby steeled her emotions against his charm, and willed herself not to think of Jesse skating with Prissy. She would do what he asked of her and be done with him—both of them. She breathed a quick prayer asking for strength to endure this trial and keep her from feeling jilted.

Jesse lowered the broom to the ice and smiled brightly. "I'm ready whenever you are."

"What's going on here?" Prissy asked with an accusatory tone.

How had she managed to sneak up on them a second time? Ruby chided herself for being so wrapped up in Jesse's masculine facade that she'd missed Prissy's approach.

"I'm teaching him to skate," Ruby said, this time through gritted teeth.

Priscilla smiled knowingly at Jesse. "Teach him well, Ruby." Priscilla looped her hands in the lapel of Jesse's navy, wool coat. "I don't want him falling on me during the Christmas Skate Party on Saturday."

With a flirtatious wink, she skated off, her ankles wobbling on the uneven surface of the frozen pond. Ruby couldn't look at Jesse. It was obvious there was something going on between the two of them. Why hadn't he asked Prissy to teach him to skate? She wasn't a bad skater—not as accomplished as Ruby, but she would have been able to teach him the basics. Ruby suddenly felt used, but she'd already agreed to teach Jesse, and now she wished she hadn't.

Jesse followed her as she went over to the wooden bench at the far end of the pond and sat to remove her skates. It would be easier to teach him if they were both wearing boots.

Bending down, Jesse grabbed the laces on her skate. "Let me help you with that."

Too shocked to argue, Ruby watched Jesse untie the laces of her skates and pull them off her feet. Why was he being so nice to her? Because he was getting free lessons from her? Nonetheless, her skin tingled at his touch, and she worried he could sense that his attention was sending her the wrong idea about their new arrangement.

Jesse cupped her stocking feet in his strong hands.

"Your feet are already freezing. Would you rather wait until tomorrow?"

Ruby was tempted to pull her feet away, but somehow couldn't. "My feet are always cold. I'm used to it and love to skate, so it goes along with the sacrifice I make for the sake of being able to enjoy the ice."

"Why do you do it? Skate, I mean…why is it so important to you?" He held fast to her toes, determined to warm her up before returning to the ice.

Ruby gulped down the lump in her throat. No one had ever asked her why she was so passionate about skating. Was he really interested, or just passing the time so he could flirt with her? If caught, his actions could be misinterpreted, but at the moment, she didn't care.

"*Mei mamm* started teaching me to skate when I was three years old. She died just after I finished school. When I skate, it makes me feel closer to her."

Jesse looked up at her with solemn eyes. She could see sincerity in them that was never there before. Was it possible that he was different from the friends he ran around with?

"Was your *mamm* a *gut* skater like you are?"

Ruby smiled, unable to help herself as she gazed upon his sparkling blue eyes and dimples that tempted her to kiss his cheeks.

"*Nee,* she was much more graceful than I am out on the ice. When she would skate, it was like she was one with the ice—like she had been born with skates on. That's what *mei daed* used to say to her."

Jesse smiled, but a shadow suddenly blocked out the sun.

Prissy stood with hands on her hips, her lips forming a disappointing line. "What is going on here?"

Chapter Four

Ruby abruptly pulled her feet from Jesse's grasp as he stood at attention. "We didn't see you walk up," he stammered.

Priscilla scowled at him. "Apparently not! What do you think you're doing touching Ruby's feet like that?"

Jesse cleared his throat. "I was trying to warm up her feet—they were cold as the icy pond."

Darting her attention between them, Prissy looked on the verge of throwing a big tantrum as she often did when things were not going her way. "Why are you even talking to her? You're supposed to be learning to skate, and that should *not* involve any touching!"

Shocked by her question and agitated by Prissy's rudeness, Ruby stuffed her feet in her cold boots and stood to face her accuser. "I was about to teach him how to skate. My feet were cold. Not that it is any of your business!"

Priscilla pursed her lips and deepened her scowl. "I didn't know that teaching someone to skate involved that much—touching!"

Jesse moved between them. "I was only trying to warm her up so we could get started on the skating lessons. I don't want to embarrass myself at the Christmas party on Saturday."

Prissy's countenance changed suddenly as she cupped her hand in the crook of Jesse's elbow. "I can't wait to skate with you." Then she turned her gaze sharply on Ruby. "Stick to the lessons and stop acting improperly or I will have a talk with your *daed.*"

Stunned by Prissy's statement, Ruby couldn't find her voice. Her mind whirled with several things to say, but the words would not form on her tongue. Had Jesse already asked Prissy to accompany him to the Christmas party? If so, why wasn't *she* teaching him how to skate? Was he mocking her by asking her to teach him?

If only I hadn't agreed to teach him to skate. At least it's only a week away. After that, I won't ever have to talk to either of them again!

✳✳✳✳

Jesse felt like he couldn't catch a break with Ruby. Every time he had a chance to be alone with her, Priscilla interrupted them. If she thought he would skate with her at the party on Saturday, she was sadly mistaken. He wanted nothing to do with the likes of her. She was rude and bossy, and he didn't like the way she spoke to Ruby. But he could hardly reprimand Priscilla without offending Ruby. They were cousins after all, and he wouldn't do anything to upset his chances for taking Ruby to the skate party.

First, he had to master the basics of skating so he wouldn't embarrass himself—or her for that matter. Then he would worry about inviting her— once he was able to stay up on the skates without ending up flat on the ice. He had a lot to live up to if he wanted to be her skate partner for the evening. Surely she would not want to skate at a party with him if she would have to spend the entire evening holding him up. Or worse—if he caused her to fall. Being an expert skater, she would feel bogged down by his amateur skills. He hadn't put on a pair of skates since he was in school, and even then, his *daed* had told him it was a waste of his time. There were always chores to be done and other things around the farm that were more important than pursuing a hobby.

To Jesse, it was not just a hobby. He enjoyed being on the ice—even if he wasn't very skilled at it. His *daed's* scolding had stuck with him, leaving him only to admire Ruby's ability over the years. He'd tried not to envy the freedom he saw in her as she would glide effortlessly across the ice. Up until now, he hadn't had the nerve to approach her for lessons, but he knew it was the only way to get close to her.

He had been enamored with her since before he'd left school. Being two grades above her, he had left his school-boy crush at school when he'd graduated. After she finished school, he'd begun to see her in a different light, and each year that passed, his feelings for her grew from crush to admiration, and finally, a possible romantic interest. He owed it to himself to explore those feelings he felt for her to be sure they were real and not just something he'd built up in his head over the years. His only worry was that she would not return his affection.

He'd been dubbed as rude and critical, as his friends could be sometimes. He had gained the reputation by the actions of those so-called friends, and he often wondered himself why he didn't find some new friends. He never went along with their constant teasing of others, but he'd never made an attempt at stopping them either, which made him guilty by association. He guessed that was why Priscilla had taken a liking to him. She would be better suited for one of his "friends" than with him, and she had gotten in the way of him getting closer with Ruby ever since she'd moved to their community. It was even more now that he'd finally been able to approach Ruby.

It was time for Jesse to make his move and find a way around Priscilla's meddling. He wanted to be Ruby's beau by Christmas, and the only way that was going to happen was if he could ask her to the skating party. The only problem would be to offset Priscilla, who was always vying for his attention. He hoped that spending time with Ruby over the next week would bring them closer together, but it would backfire on him if he couldn't find a way to divert Priscilla's attention away from him. He needed a plan to get closer to Ruby without having Priscilla in the way. Jesse liked Ruby, and he hoped she felt the same way about him.

Chapter Five

"Please, Tobias, I'll do your chores for a month if you keep Priscilla busy while I skate with Ruby!"

Tobias looked at his older *bruder* with skepticism. "What are you going to do when *daed* finds out what you're up to? If he sees you doing my chores, we'll be in trouble for sure and for certain."

Jesse was growing impatient. "*Daed* won't find out. Please say you'll help me!"

Tobias stopped fluffing the hay in the horse stall and leaned against the pitchfork in his hands.

"The way I see it, there's two problems with that plan of yours."

"What would those be?" Jesse interrupted him.

"Well, first off," Tobias began. "I don't see how either of us will have time to do *any* chores if we're busy skating with those two every day. Secondly, Priscilla doesn't like me—she likes you!"

Jesse let out a sigh, his breath visible in the cold barn. "I think she is expecting me to ask her to the Christmas Skate Party, and I want to take Ruby. That's why I'm trying to learn how to skate."

Tobias glared at his *bruder.* "I hope that doesn't mean you expect me to take Priscilla to the skate party. I don't like her!"

"I'm not asking you to like her—just keep her away from me and Ruby for a few days so I can get to know Ruby better."

Glaring at Jesse, Tobias set his pitchfork back in motion. "I won't make you do my chores, but if I ever need a favor, you will have to do it—no questions asked!"

Jesse patted Tobias on the shoulder. "I will do that, little *bruder.* "

✳✳✳✳

"I wouldn't be surprised if Jesse asked me to the skate party when we arrive at the Christmas Singing tonight. He was hinting at it when he took me home the other night," Prissy said as she helped Ruby pack the remainder of the gingerbread cookies for the Singing.

Ruby narrowed her eyes. She didn't want to be put in the middle of a relationship between Prissy and Jesse. "What about his *bruder,* Tobias? He seemed interested in you when we were at the pond yesterday."

Prissy turned up her nose. "He's nice enough, but he's kind of young, don't you think?"

Ruby rolled her eyes. "He's our age, Prissy!"

"I know that, Ruby, but I prefer a *mann* who is more mature—like Jesse."

Ruby knew she wasn't going to win this argument, so she gave up. "Gabriel's waiting for us with the sleigh. We should probably get out there before he goes to the singing without us."

Prissy pushed by her without another word.

It was going to be a long night.

✳✳✳✳

"Let's go, Eden," Jesse hollered from the back door. "We're going to be late."

Eden was so excited to be attending her first Christmas Singing—even if she had to attend with both of her *bruders.* She'd never been able to attend before, but because she had her heart set on Ruby's older *bruder,* Gabriel, she was eager to attend. She worried that her twin *bruder,* Tobias was taking an interest in bossy-Prissy, and hoped she would not be there—for the sake of Tobias *and* Ruby.

Pushing her worry aside, her excitement renewed and she wanted to be certain she looked presentable. With her best dress on, she felt confident in the pink one that complimented her blue eyes. Her blond hair was tucked neatly beneath her *kapp,* and she stole one last glance in the mirror before Jesse announced he was leaving without her if she didn't come out of the washroom.

She'd waited too long to be left behind.

"I'm ready," Eden hollered back as she entered the kitchen. "Please don't go without me."

Jesse stood at the kitchen door smiling at his younger *schweschder*. "I can't believe you're so grown up."

Eden shrugged past him. "Don't embarrass me by making a big deal out of this. I could have gone for a few years now—if *Daed* would have let me go."

"Do you have your mittens?" their *mudder* called after her.

"*Jah. Guten nacht, mamm,*" Eden answered over her shoulder. She was too excited to kiss her *mamm,* fearing it would increase the lump in her throat.

Excitement flared in her as she stepped into the waiting sleigh. She covered herself with the lap-quilt, not feeling the cold at all. Her *bruders* sat in front, leaving her feeling very important to be escorted to her first Christmas Singing. Snowflakes touched her warm cheeks as the horses set the sleigh in motion. The jingling of their harness bells kept her mind only on Gabriel and the events of the night before her. She would put all her worries aside for this one special night so that she could enjoy every aspect of it.

Ruby walked ahead of Priscilla as she looked for her best friend, Eden Fisher, while Gabriel tied up the horses. When Ruby spotted her, she was delighted that she could share her friend's first Christmas Singing experience with her. They approached each other and squealed with delight. Priscilla sat down after scowling at the two of them. Ruby was glad she'd left them alone; she didn't like having her cousin tag along all the time.

"Prissy doesn't look happy to see me," Eden said. "What's her problem?"

Ruby waved a hand at her. "Who cares what she thinks. She's mad at me because your *bruder* asked me to teach him how to skate."

Eden's eyes grew wide. "Tobias?"

Ruby shook her head cautiously. "*Nee.* It was Jesse who asked me."

Eden was happy for her friend since she knew Jesse was sweet on her, but they hadn't discussed it much. She still thought it best to keep quiet until Ruby found out for herself if it was what she hoped.

"That's *wunderbaar,* Ruby. But why do you look so glum?"

Ruby looked at the floor. "Because I think he wants to learn so he can ask Prissy to the skate party on Saturday."

Eden looked at her friend, wondering if she should quell her fears with her suspicions, or if it would hurt her more if she was wrong about Jesse's intentions.

It's probably better if I wait, Eden thought. *Gott, please be with Ruby and Jesse. If it is your will, bring them together in love...and forgive me for not wanting mei bruder to fall in lieb with Prissy!*

Chapter Six

Jesse met up with his friend, Gabe, Ruby's *bruder,* outside the Yoder's barn. Though he was eager to see Ruby tonight at the Christmas Singing, he wasn't looking forward to the lecture he would surely get from his friend regarding his interest in his *schweschder.* He knew that Gabriel had taken an interest in his younger *schweschder,* Eden, and hoped it would help to smooth things over between them when his feelings for Ruby were discussed.

I couldn't find a better suitor for Eden than Gabe. He's a gut mann, and it would be nice to have a friend as a bruder-in-law. But would he feel the same about me if I expressed my interest in his younger schweschder? Perhaps I should wait to mention it since he has so much on his own plate right now.

Gabe patted Jesse on the shoulder. "I hear you asked Ruby to teach you to skate."

Here we go…Gott, give me the strength to endure his disapproval, and please don't let my interest in Ruby cause a rift between Gabe and me.

"*Jah.* She is the best in the community, and I'd like to attend the Christmas Skate on Saturday—and not just to watch."

"You know the rest of the guys are going to tease you for skating. They did it to me."

Jesse shrugged. "They aren't really our friends anyway, are they? They like to make trouble and tease everyone, and I think we've outgrown a few of them since we left school so many years ago, don't you?"

Gabriel nodded. "I was only tolerating them because I thought you didn't want to upset your cousin, Henry."

"*Nee,*" Jesse said. "Those are all Henry's friends, and I'm tired of them hanging around. Perhaps it's time I had a talk with him. They are taking their *rumspringa* to a far more rebellious level than I'm comfortable with, and I wish Henry would stop hanging out with them."

"Now that it's out in the open, if you need help talking to him, I'll help you," Gabriel offered.

"Thanks, Gabe. I appreciate it."

They walked toward the Yoder's barn where the singing had already begun.

"About *mei schweschder…*"

"Gabe, I thought we had settled that part of the conversation. She's teaching me to skate. Is that alright with you?"

Gabriel punched Jesse in the arm playfully.

"Don't break her heart."

"But…" Jesse started to say.

Gabriel chuckled. "You don't have to say a word. I can see it in your eyes."

Gabriel figured it was better to let his friend off the hook, hoping that when it came time to tell Jesse of his *real* intentions toward his *schweschder,* Eden, he would be as lenient with him.

✳✳✳✳

Ruby spotted Jesse the moment he walked into the barn, as though she somehow sensed his presence. The hair on the back of her neck prickled as their eyes met. How was she going to get through a real skate lesson with Jesse without falling for him? Knowing it was best to guard her heart from reality didn't make it any easier to think of him asking Prissy to the Christmas party instead of her. She shook the thought away as Jesse's smile warmed her heart. Even from this distance, she could feel something more than friendship from him—was she reading more into his smile than he intended?

Prissy rushed to her side. "Stop smiling at Jesse, Ruby, or he'll think you're interested in him. You wouldn't want to do anything to mess up my chances with him, would you?"

"Leave her alone, Prissy," Eden said. "If *mei bruder* wants to smile at Ruby, you can't do anything about it. He can like whoever he wants to like."

Priscilla turned up her nose. "I will have to tell him to act properly while you're teaching him to skate. We wouldn't want people getting the wrong impression about the two of you."

"Leave it alone, Prissy," Eden warned. "You can't control who people like, no matter how much you try. Your actions are making you look bad, so you might want to sit down and be quiet. Act respectable or *you* will be the one everyone is talking about!"

Priscilla walked away from them, a scowl of defeat creasing her brow.

Eden turned to Ruby. "Why do you let her push you around like that?"

"She seems desperate to get married and wants to be the center of attention. She has been lying to *mei daed* for weeks trying to get me into trouble. He knows she is lying and hasn't disciplined me, but Prissy is doing everything she can to get me out of the way so she can be the most popular. I'm not trying to be more popular than she is, be she feels threatened because I am well liked and she has become known in the community by her sour reputation."

Eden hugged Ruby. "I'm glad your *daed* believes you. But I sure wish she would leave you alone. You haven't done anything to deserve to be treated that way by her—except be nicer than she is. We need to keep her in our prayers so she will leave you alone."

"What will I do if Jesse doesn't ask her to the skating party? Prissy will blame me for sure and for certain."

Eden giggled, knowing the real reason for her friend's distress was that she, herself, wanted to be the one Jesse asked. "You leave Prissy up to me. I will find her a distraction so you can teach *mei bruder* to skate without her breathing down the back of your neck the entire time."

"I have a confession to make," Ruby said.

Giggling more, Eden laid a comforting hand on Ruby's shoulder. "I already know you want to court Jesse—I have a feeling he feels the same way about you too!"

Ruby began to shake. If what her friend said was true, then his request to teach him to skate was an excuse to get closer to her. How was she going to keep her head on straight and teach him without falling to pieces?

Chapter Seven

Ruby was nervous knowing Prissy's eyes had not left her and Jesse the entire time they'd been on the ice. She was nervous enough with Jesse holding onto her to keep from falling, without having Prissy's angry glare burning a hole in her back. But when she felt a sudden change in that sinking feeling, she sought out Prissy's whereabouts to confirm the shift in her feelings. Eden's twin, Tobias had approached Prissy, and Ruby struggled to watch them.

"Are you going to watch your cousin all day, or are you going to concentrate on what you're doing so we don't fall on the ice?"

Jesse's question startled Ruby.

"I asked *mei bruder* to keep her busy for me so I could concentrate on learning to skate," he said.

Ruby tipped her skates sideways, bringing them both to an abrupt stop. "Maybe this wasn't such a *gut* idea. Prissy obviously wants to be the one to teach you to skate. She doesn't even want me talking to you."

Jesse smiled, nearly bringing Ruby to her knees. "Well that isn't up to her, now, is it?"

Ruby shook her head mechanically, lost in the smoky baritone of Jesse's voice, and the nearness of him made her feel warm.

Jesse smoothed his hand briefly over her arm.

"I asked you to teach me, and Priscilla will have to learn she can't be the center of attention all the time. She isn't the best skater in the community— you are."

His compliment brought heat to Ruby's cheeks. Was it possible she had his intentions for her all wrong? She didn't dare hope that Jesse liked her as much as she liked him. His gentle affections would suggest he returned her feelings, but she would push it aside until he made it clear to her what those feelings were.

"You seem to have the gliding down, but you need to work on keeping your ankles straight."

Jesse grabbed onto her arm and straightened his ankles. "It's easy to do if we are just standing here, but once we start to skate, they get wobbly again."

Ruby tried to keep from giggling. "We also need to work on your posture. You have a tendency to lean forward instead of standing upright."

Without thinking, Ruby placed a hand on his chest and back. "If you remain upright, there is less chance of falling. You need to keep this trunk of yours strong."

His muscular chest could be felt easily enough beneath her mitten-clad hands, and she quickly let go of him when she realized she was touching him.

Jesse grabbed her hand that she'd removed from his chest and held it for a minute. She met his gaze with anticipation, only to have the spell break as they both tumbled to the ice.

Ruby grabbed her ankle that twisted beneath Jesse and cried out in pain. Rising to his knees, he pulled off her skate as quickly as he could to examine her ankle. She was in so much pain she couldn't properly enjoy the attention Jesse paid to her. He was speaking gently to her, but she didn't really hear him.

"I don't think it's broken, but we should get you over to the doctor immediately. Let me grab my boots over at the bench and I'll be right back."

Jesse was back at her side in no time. Scooping her up into his strong arms, Ruby was not shy in leaning against the strong plane of his chest. He cradled her gently as he carried her to the far side of the pond where all the other youth had gathered to warm themselves at the outdoor fireplace.

Gabriel came running toward them. "What happened?"

"We slipped on the ice," Jesse told her *bruder*. "She twisted her ankle under me."

Jesse handed her over to Gabriel, and she was sad to leave the safety of Jesse's arms. "She should go see the doc right away."

Prissy turned to Jesse. "Will you take me home?"

Jesse nodded, and the look of satisfaction on Prissy's face was enough to churn Ruby's stomach. Ruby knew that her cousin would take full advantage of her unfortunate circumstance and turn it around for her own benefit. There was nothing to do about it but pray she would have patience to tolerate her cousin's unkindness. She loved Prissy, but lately, she didn't much like her at all.

Gabriel placed Ruby in the back of his sleigh and placed a lap-quilt over her to keep her warm. Jesse rushed up to the sleigh with her other skate and her boots. As he handed them to her, the look of sorrow in his eyes nearly made Ruby weep, but she swallowed down the painful lump that nearly choked her.

"I'm sorry," he barely whispered.

Ruby laid a hand on his arm. "I know," she said, her bottom lip quivering.

She longed to be back in his arms, but she couldn't be certain his kindness wasn't out of guilt for making her fall. Though just before they'd fallen, she'd thought she'd seen a glimmer of interest in his eyes, but she didn't dare hope for such a thing.

Gabriel clicked to the horses, and the sleigh's runners skimmed across the fresh snow. The last thing Ruby saw was Jesse helping a very eager Prissy into the front seat of his sleigh, and then he climbed in next to her.

Ruby tried to erase the image from her mind, not wanting to believe that the two of them were a couple, but from the look of it, it appeared to be that way. It upset Ruby that Prissy didn't get in the back of Jesse's sleigh with Eden, but if she knew Prissy, she would have insisted on riding up front with Jesse for the appearance it gave Ruby and everyone else.

Chapter Eight

"Jesse asked *me* to finish teaching him how to skate," Prissy boasted.

Ruby didn't want to believe Jesse would do such a thing, but if Prissy was about to go meet with him, then it must be true.

"When you think about it, Ruby, it makes the most sense. I don't know why Jesse didn't ask me in the first place. It's obvious I'm a better skater than you are. After all, I wouldn't have fallen the way you did."

Ruby bit her bottom lip to keep from retorting out of anger. It didn't matter what Prissy said about her—she knew the truth.

"You could have spared yourself the embarrassment," Prissy continued. "If you had simply told Jesse when he asked you that I was the better choice to teach him what he needed to know."

Ruby didn't like the slyness of Prissy's statement. It implied improper behavior, and she didn't want to think about Prissy throwing herself at Jesse the way she was. If he held Prissy while they skated the way he had held her yesterday, Ruby was certain she would cry. But what did it matter? She was incapable of skating with him now. The doctor said she had to be off her feet for two full days. In two days, Prissy could have Jesse talked into marrying her! Ruby hoped Jesse wasn't that fickle, but she knew Prissy was *that* pushy. Besides, Jesse was probably better suited for Prissy; they were both bold and outspoken, and Ruby was too timid and shy.

Tugging the quilt up to her neck, Ruby reclined on the sofa in the sitting room and turned her back on her cousin. "I need to rest, Prissy."

Priscilla sighed heavily. "I can take a hint, Ruby. You don't want me around because you're jealous of me!"

She stormed off without another word.

Ruby wasn't jealous, she was simply tired of Prissy belittling her and trying to provoke her. If she was going to be with Jesse, it would be *Gotte's Wille*, and there would be nothing Ruby could do about it. She would *not* waste time arguing with Prissy, who seemed to delight in her agony; her time would be better spent in prayer. She would pray an unselfish prayer for Prissy's happiness, as well as her own and Jesse's. The rest was up to *Gott,* and Ruby was determined to accept whatever was in store for her future—with or without Jesse Fisher.

✳✳✳✳

"This isn't going to work, Priscilla," Jesse said impatiently. "I appreciate your offer to help me, but I'd rather skate alone and work on the things Ruby already taught me before…"

"Before you knocked her down and probably crippled her for life," Priscilla barked. "You should be ashamed of yourself for pushing her!"

Jesse finished lacing up his skate and stood up, towering over Priscilla. "That was an accident, and you know it, Priscilla."

Prissy folded her arms and held her ground.

"Tell that to Ruby!"

Jesse tried his best to keep his emotions from surfacing, but he just couldn't. "Does Ruby blame me for the accident?"

The corners of Prissy's mouth turned up with contempt. "Of course she blames you; she might never skate again!"

Jesse squared his shoulders and pushed past her onto the ice. He breathed a simple prayer as he moved his way toward the end of the pond where Ruby had fallen—where he'd caused her to fall. He couldn't bear to think that he could be responsible for her never being able to skate again. Tears erupted in his throat, threatening to flood his vision. How could he possibly make this up to her?

Without realizing it, Jesse skated a perfect *figure-eight*, tracing the grooves left in the ice from Ruby the day before. He straightened, holding his frame the way she'd told him to, as he skated almost perfectly across the ice.

He'd never felt so free.

Then it dawned on him; Ruby had taught him everything except what he now realized. She'd instructed him on the basics of keeping his back and his ankles straight, and how to glide. But now as he glided over the sleek surface of the pond, he'd finally learned the one lesson no one can teach: the love of the ice. It was as if he finally understood what Ruby had told him about her connection to the ice and how it made her feel.

When Ruby skated, it was like watching a dandelion seedling floating around atop the tall grasses in the field. She danced across the ice with such grace and elegance; he couldn't help but desire that feeling. Now, in her absence, he understood her passion. He had taken that away from her when he'd caused her to fall. It was her connection to her *mamm*, and if she could never skate again, she might never forgive him for losing something so precious to her. Jesse's heart swelled with love for Ruby. He ached for her potential loss.

Gott, please heal Ruby's ankle. Restore her ability to skate, and preserve the connection she feels with her mamm when she's skating. Help her to forgive me for causing her to fall.

✳✳✳✳

Ruby could not get comfortable no matter what she did. Eden had stayed with her most of the afternoon and brought her hot tea and gingerbread cookies, but nothing made Ruby happy. She was miserable—not because of the little bit of pain left in her ankle, but because of the stabbing pain in her heart. She hadn't realized until it was too late that she loved Jesse, and the thought of having to give him up made her heart ache. She didn't dare share her feelings with Eden. After all, how do you tell your best friend that you're in love with her *bruder*—especially when you know there is no way he will ever return those feelings? She wasn't willing to make a fool of herself any more than she already had. It was always best to keep quiet regarding things that would cause potential embarrassment. She would hold it all in and wait for *Gott* to heal the hurt.

Chapter Nine

"But Eden, you must know something! You're her best friend."

Jesse was pleading with his *schweschder,* when he should have tried harder to make Ruby see him. He'd tried to pay her a visit, but her *daed* had turned him away, explaining that Ruby had no desire to accept his visit. The only explanation was that she blamed him for the fall and refused to forgive him.

"Just because we are friends doesn't mean I know everything she is thinking. She was very sad when I was with her yesterday. When I see her this afternoon, I will try to get through to her. I know you care for her, but it's probably best not to push her right now."

Jesse didn't like that answer. The only thing that would satisfy his guilt was knowing she was able to skate again. If he'd taken that away from her, he would never be able to live with himself. He set his *kaffi* cup in the sink and shrugged into his coat. He had chores to do if he was going to make time to practice out on the pond later this afternoon.

✳✳✳✳

Ruby fought back tears as she silently prayed that Prissy was telling lies about her relationship with Jesse. She had become quite the liar, and Ruby hoped she was lying about this too. If Jesse had indeed asked Prissy to the Christmas Skate Party on Saturday, then Ruby had no reason to push her recovery. Yesterday, she'd wanted to be up on her feet again so she could skate with Jesse. But after hearing Prissy's announcement just now, she would stay as far away from the pond on Saturday as she could. No use in making a fool of herself when Jesse didn't want her. He'd made his choice and Ruby would have to live with it.

"I'm on my way to skate with him again this afternoon," Prissy announced. "He's really improving now that I've begun to help him. I suppose if you'd taught him the right way then he wouldn't have fallen, and you wouldn't be laying on the sofa feeling sorry for yourself."

She wasn't feeling sorry for herself; her heart was broken, and her cousin was rubbing her misfortune in her face. "You obviously didn't come here to see how I was faring, so please leave. I'm not feeling up to having visitors."

Gabriel entered the sitting room with an armful of wood for the fireplace. "Be on your way, Priscilla."

Ruby was suddenly grateful for her *bruder's* authoritative support. It made her realize that he, too, had recognized Prissy's presence as a nuisance. Priscilla left promptly after shooting an angry glare in Ruby's direction.

"Why do you let her push you around like that, Ruby?" Gabriel asked.

Ruby shrugged. "I suppose I feel sorry for her. Besides, she's *familye.*"

Gabriel placed two logs on the fire and stirred up the coals to ignite them. "*Jah,* except she needs to remember her manners."

Ruby knew better than to say anything more about the subject, and she was content to let the matter drop. She snuggled deeper under the quilt until the fire spread warmth into the room. Alone with her thoughts, Ruby whispered a prayer of forgiveness for feelings of anger toward Prissy and Jesse. She knew it wasn't fair to begrudge them true happiness if that was *Gotte's Wille.*

✳✳✳✳

"She's lying, Ruby," Eden said. "She spent the entire afternoon skating with Tobias."

Ruby tested her ankle before putting her full weight on it. Satisfied that she could walk to the other room without limping, Ruby knew her ankle would be strong enough by the following day to get back out onto the ice. "Jesse told me he asked Tobias to keep her occupied while we skated. I guess I thought he meant to keep her away from the other *menner* so he could have Prissy for himself as his date for the party."

Eden shook her head with disgust. "You know *mei bruder* isn't like that, Ruby."

"I know, and I'm sorry. Prissy was just here an hour ago trying to convince me that Jesse asked her to the Christmas Skate Party. Why would she do that?"

"Because she's a spiteful, mean liar," Eden said through gritted teeth.

"*Nee,* she's hurting the same as I was after *mei mamm* died. She and her *mamm* were forced to come here and live after her *daed* and *bruder* died in the buggy accident. She is jealous of *mei familye—mei daed* and *bruders.*"

"That doesn't make any sense. You're both missing a parent," Eden said.

"She was never like this when we were younger. Do you remember two summers ago when she last visited? We had a lot of fun. And then—the accident happened with her *familye.*"

"I suppose it makes sense. I don't remember her ever being this mean." Eden agreed. "What can we do to make her stop acting this way?"

Ruby took Eden's hands in hers and squeezed lightly. "We show her mercy."

Eden knew Ruby was right, even if she didn't know how much mercy she could show a person who was as mean-spirited as Prissy. But for her best friend,

Eden was willing to try—and for the sake of Jesse. There was also Gabriel to consider, the one with whom Eden was interested in sharing some time on the ice at the Christmas party, and possibly more.

Chapter Ten

Snowflakes fell like glitter from the sky as Ruby twirled around the ice. She'd finished her chores early, hoping to have some solitude on the ice before the rest of the youth began to gather for the last practice before the skate party that would be underway later that evening. She'd avoided Prissy after her announcement that she would be attending the skate party with Jesse. She expected them to arrive late so Prissy could be sure everyone could see her shallow victory—Jesse being her prize. Prissy didn't love Jesse, and it didn't seem fair that she should win his heart. But Ruby was determined to abide by *Gotte's Wille.*

Letting the scraping of her skates across the surface of the ice lull her into the past, Ruby longed to have her *mamm* beside her, holding her hand the way she used to when she was young.

"I was hoping to find you here," Jesse's familiar voice startled her.

She came to an abrupt stop, the blades of her skates spraying ice on him. "Sorry," she said with a smile.

"You'd think I'd learn to steer clear from you when you're stopping suddenly, but I suppose I will need to be sprayed with ice shavings a few more times before it will sink in."

Silence formed a barrier between them as she rolled slowly toward the edge of the pond where Jesse stood, his gaze reeling her in toward him. He sat on the bench and began to lace up his skates while she swished back and forth in front of him. She didn't dare ask why he was looking for her, and she didn't dare hope it was to ask her to the skate party. With only a few hours until the party, she knew she would be attending with Gabriel and Eden. Tobias would likely go with them so Jesse could escort Prissy in his sleigh. Ruby was determined to be happy for her cousin, and she would be content to skate with Eden. With any luck, one of the young *menner* in the youth group would ask her to skate—and she would be happy about it.

Really she would.

Jesse suddenly surprised Ruby by skating up behind her and pulled her into a *figure-eight*. It wasn't perfect, but it was far more graceful than she'd expected.

She looked into his eyes as the trees around the pond wished by them. "You knew how to skate all along! You tricked me!"

"*Nee,* I didn't trick you. It wasn't my first time on skates, and I'd forgotten how to balance and keep my ankles straight, but I learned *this* from watching you over the years. Earlier today when I let myself go, and imagined—the way you probably do—I was able to skate better. This is because of the way I feel about you, Ruby."

They both stopped and Jesse faced her. "I'm sorry for making you fall, but if that hadn't happened, I probably would not have had the time on the ice to sort out how I feel."

"I forgive you, Jesse." She didn't dare say anymore, or hope he would reveal he felt the same about her as she felt about him. She loved him. There was no doubt as she gazed into his blue eyes, his crooked smile inviting her closer.

Just when she thought she couldn't take the suspense anymore, Jesse pulled off his gloves and cupped her face with his hands. He lifted her face gently toward him until his cold lips touched hers, warming them with the love he felt for her. Ruby was lost in his kiss, the gentle sweeping of his mouth across hers sent shivers straight to her toes.

Jesse pulled away from the kiss. "Will you be my date for the Christmas party tonight? I apologize for asking at the last minute and would have asked you sooner, but you wouldn't see me."

"*Jah,*" she said with a giggle.

Ruby could hardly contain her emotions. It was *her* that Jesse liked. She had been wrong about Jesse's interest in her and couldn't be happier about it.

"What is going on here?" Prissy interrupted.

Ruby's heart thumped forcefully against her ribcage. She had been wrong about Prissy too, and she owed her an apology for assuming the worst about her dear cousin.

Jesse gave her hand a squeeze, letting her know it was alright to end their conversation for the time-being. "I'll pick you up at seven o'clock."

Ruby couldn't help but smile, which he returned in earnest. "I can't wait!"

He left Ruby and Priscilla and went to the bench to remove his skates.

Ruby turned to Prissy. "Before you yell at me, I want to explain."

Prissy interrupted her. "I'm sorry for the way I've been acting. I was the one that was jealous of you—for having your *daed and bruder* when mine are gone. I know you lost your *mudder,* and I was never there for you when you went through that. This is my first Christmas without *mei familye,* and I've been taking my anger out on you. Will you forgive me, Ruby?"

Tears pooled in Ruby's eyes. She hurt for her cousin. She knew how it felt to lose a parent, but not a *bruder.* Knowing the pain she'd endured at the loss of her *mamm,* she couldn't imagine having to be without Gabriel too.

"I'm sorry too, Prissy. I misjudged you, and let my feelings for Jesse cloud my vision so much that I couldn't see you were hurting and needed me."

Prissy hugged Ruby briefly. "I have something I want to tell you, but I have someone waiting for me right now. Something amazing has happened and I can't wait to tell you. Can we talk later at the party?"

Ruby was stunned.

Prissy seemed almost *happy.*

"*Jah,* I can't wait to have a talk with you about whatever it is that seems to have you in better spirits."

Prissy smiled. "It's *wunderbaar.* We will have a long talk later—the way we used to when we were young girls spending our summers together."

Ruby hugged Prissy again, a prayer of thanks on her heart.

THE END

A Novella

Chapter One

"Leave me alone, Tobias!" Priscilla shouted. "I don't want to skate with you!"

Tobias huddled up closer to Prissy. "*Mei schweschder* and *bruder* asked me to keep you company, so I have to or I will never hear the end of it from either of them."

Priscilla tipped the toe-kick forward on her right skate and dragged it across the ice until she slowed enough to face Tobias. "What do you mean they asked you to keep me company? That's why you've been skating with me for the past two days? Do they think I can't take care of myself? Do you think I'm a *boppli* and you have to watch me?"

"*Nee.* Exactly the opposite."

Prissy stared at the layer of snow gathering along the brim of Tobias's black hat. She didn't dare gaze upon the depth of his blue eyes that both frightened and excited her. Jesse was the target of her affection because there was safety in his rejection. If she let down the guard around her heart with Tobias, she might not survive the pain he would leave in his wake. Steeling her emotions against Tobias's charm, Prissy bit her bottom lip to distract herself from the hope that tried to creep into her heart.

Having just lost her *daed* and her *bruder* less than a year ago, she couldn't afford to let another *mann* into her heart. She felt so shattered by the loss that she didn't think she had any heart left to spare another person. She'd been pushing everyone away for months—especially her cousin, Ruby, who was only trying to help her. Prissy didn't want any help; she could handle her life on her own. After all, with the exception of her *mamm,* who paid little attention to her anymore, she was all alone in this world.

"The opposite of what, Tobias?" she asked through gritted teeth.

Tobias smiled at her, his breath forming an icy cloud that Prissy focused on—anything to keep from looking at him directly.

"You're anything but a *boppli.* Anyone with eyes can see what a beautiful young woman you are."

Priscilla pursed her lips and sighed. "Tobias Fisher, you are not allowed to speak to me that way!"

Tobias chuckled. "I don't see anyone stopping me!" He poked her ribs in fun, skating backward to keep himself just out of her reach. "Do you think *you* can stop me?"

Was he flirting with her or teasing her? Either way, his gentle laugh twisted her heart into knots she could not untangle. If she allowed him to disrupt her thoughts and break through the barriers that guarded her heart, there would be no turning back.

Tobias turned his mouth downward in a mock-frown. "You don't even want to try? You're no fun!"

Priscilla pushed at him, but he slid to the side and turned sharply on the ice. He was an excellent skater among other things. He was far too handsome to be considered a *buwe. Nee,* Tobias was a *mann,* and far too charming to resist.

"Is this fun for you? Skating with me because your *familye* ordered you to?"

Pushing himself in front of her, Tobias grabbed Priscilla's hands and pulled her along while he skated backward. "They aren't forcing me; I have my own will."

Prissy bit her lip to keep from arguing with Tobias. He was an above-average skater, and above average in looks too. She found it difficult to resist him when he smiled, his blue eyes reflecting the sky. Wisps of snow danced around them as their surroundings meshed together until there was only the two of them skating on the ice. Voices became muffled and scenery blurred as Tobias came into focus. His thick, blond hair was pushed back off his forehead and tucked beneath his hat. Broad shoulders framed his muscular chest that was visible through his open coat. His royal blue shirt hugged him the way Priscilla wanted to.

Steeling herself against such thoughts, Priscilla broke free from Tobias. "I have to go!"

"Please stay a little longer," he pleaded. "I'd like to get to know you better."

Fear gripped Priscilla's heart and squeezed until it brought pain. She couldn't breathe. Trees around the pond began to spin out of control. If she didn't leave, she would surely pass out.

"You look like you need to sit down," Tobias said as he urged her toward a bench on the edge of the pond.

Priscilla didn't resist for fear she would collapse in front of him and embarrass herself. She shivered, but not just from the cold. His arm around her waist made it nearly impossible for her to concentrate on the steps she took toward the bench.

"You're cold," he said. "I have a lap-quilt in the sleigh. I could even give you a ride home."

"*Nee*, I can walk," she said through chattering teeth.

"I can't let you walk home," he said in almost a whisper so close to her temple.

How had he managed to get so close without her knowing? Or had she been aware of him the whole time?

Priscilla lowered herself to the bench, sad to be out of Tobias's arms. "I'll wait here for you."

With one last smile that caused Priscilla's heart to flutter, he was gone from her side. Her gaze followed him as he lumbered across the snow toward his waiting sleigh. She couldn't sit there and wait for him; she had to leave before he invaded her heart more than he already had. There was no way Priscilla would be able to resist his charms if he continued to cradle her heart with his.

Chapter Two

Hanging the laces of her skates over her shoulder, Priscilla put a hand on the skate hanging down the front of her and hooked her gloved fingers in the gap between the blade and the boot. She was tempted to wait until Tobias returned from his sleigh to take her home, but she wasn't ready to face her feelings for him. With Tobias preoccupied with telling his *bruder,* Jesse, he was giving her a ride home; Priscilla set her own course toward home.

Every step she took away from Tobias moved her further away from the glimpse of happiness she'd just experienced. It had given her a token glimmer of hope to move forward with her life. Priscilla had been so full of anger for so many months over the loss of her *daed* and *bruder,* and she felt guilty for finding joy in anything. Would she ever be able to feel normal again? Would the pain of losing the *menner* in her *familye* ever go away?

Thick snow fell on her cheeks and she blinked heavy flakes from her dark lashes. Her emotions were not so easy to brush away. Her boots crunched with every labored step in the new-fallen snow. Her heart was heavy and her footfalls heavier. Why had she walked away from Tobias? He was kind, and much more handsome than Jesse. So why was she fixating so much on Jesse when it was clear he wanted nothing to do with her? The only reason she could give herself was that it was easier to go after something she knew she couldn't get than to admit fear over rejection from the one she did want—Tobias.

Tiring of walking already, Priscilla stumbled off the side of the path and crumpled to the ground. Without thinking, her arms and legs made wide arcs to form a snow angel. Tears welled up in her throat as she continued to form the snow angel. Snowflakes fell on her as though she was one with the earth, and she was numb from the snow melting beneath her, soaking her dress and thick stockings. Priscilla closed her eyes against the falling snow, her sobs shaking her. She didn't care that the thick snow buried her in a cold cocoon that would soon smother her.

Gott, I miss mei daed and mei bruder.

✻✻✻✻

Tobias had watched Prissy wander from the bench where he'd left her as he struggled to untie the knots in the laces of his ice skates. If he couldn't get his boots on in a hurry, he'd lose sight of her before he could catch up to her. He didn't want her walking home alone after the way she looked a few minutes before. He felt responsible, but more than that, he realized he cared for her. He had no idea how it happened, or even when, since up until a few days ago he'd spent very little time around her.

Stuffing his feet into his boots, Tobias hopped from the *familye* sleigh and searched the path for Priscilla. The snow was too thick and the wind too fierce for him to see any sign of her. He tucked his scarf into the collar of his wool coat and walked toward the path, wondering if it would help to call out her name. Deciding against it, he whispered a prayer for guidance in locating her. Shielding his eyes from the sting of the thickening snow, Tobias prayed she'd already made her way home.

Up ahead, something to the side of the path caught his eye.

It was Priscilla—lying on the ground.

He rushed to her, worrying she had collapsed. When he drew closer, he could barely distinguish the outline of a snow angel surrounding her lifeless form. Falling to his knees beside her, Tobias scooped her head out of the snow, and gently swept the ice from her cheeks with his bare hand.

She groaned.

At least she was alive, and had not been lying there long enough to risk frostbite. Pulling her into his arms, Tobias stood, her tiny frame cradled against him.

"My snow angel," Priscilla mumbled.

Tobias placed a kiss on her forehead that rested against his chest. "You can finish it later," he said gently.

"I have to make one for *mei bruder.*"

"You already made one," Tobias answered her.

"That was for *mei daed.* He's in heaven."

Tobias felt his heart thump double-time. She was making snow angels for her deceased *familye*—no wonder she was delirious. He couldn't imagine how much she must have been hurting to risk her own safety to do such a thing.

With no further response from her, Tobias braced the two of them against the wind and carried her slowly toward the doctor's *haus.* His home office was closer than Priscilla's farm, and Tobias worried she needed tending to.

Priscilla suddenly wriggled in his arms. "Put me down!" she demanded.

"I'm taking you to see the doctor," Tobias said firmly. "If the doc says you're alright, then I'll let you walk on your own."

Pushing at his chest, Tobias fought to hold onto to her. "I'm telling you I'm alright. I don't need to see the doctor."

Tobias stopped walking; Priscilla's struggling against him making his steps difficult in the deep snow. He looked into her pale face that was so close to his. He was tempted to kiss her shivering lips just to quiet them.

"You were passed out in the snow and you were deliriously talking about snow angels. I think you need to see the doc."

Priscilla wriggled from his arms, her feet hitting the ground with a muffled thump in the deep snow. She studied Tobias, wondering how much she'd revealed to him without knowing.

"Mind your own business, Tobias Fisher, and stay out of mine. Next time you think you need to go rescuing someone, leave me alone because I don't want your help, and I certainly don't need it!"

Tobias watched Priscilla walk away from him, dragging his heart along with every step she took.

Chapter Three

Tobias wondered if he was doing the right thing as he stepped into Priscilla's yard. It was late, but he felt compelled to finish for her what she had started and failed to do earlier that day. He had heard that she and her *mudder* had moved to the community after her *daed* and *bruder* had died in a buggy accident. He couldn't imagine what she must be feeling from her loss. More than that, this would be her first Christmas without her whole *familye,* and Tobias decided to make it his personal goal to make her Christmas as happy as possible—even if that meant enduring a lot more of her yelling at him.

By the light of the moon, Tobias lowered himself onto the glistening snow and began the first snow angel. He had not made one of these since he was a young *buwe,* but he was certain he remembered how. Moving his legs and arms in a perfect arc, he swished the deep snow to form the first angel. As he lay on the ground in the stillness of the crisp, night air, Tobias let his thoughts wander to Priscilla. It had been nice to hold her earlier, even if she had resisted him when she'd opened her green eyes and looked at him. The temptation to kiss her had been too great to resist, but he did for her sake.

Tobias stood up carefully so he didn't mess up the formation of the snow angel. He looked down at it, wondering if he should trample it and leave or if he should risk angering Priscilla by making a second one. He hoped they would cheer her up, but he knew there was a chance his efforts would backfire on him. Priscilla was moody to say the least, and he only wished she would let him comfort her and ease the pain of her loss. Instead, she let her anger spill over to everyone around her. Tobias wasn't worried about himself so much as he was about her. She was quickly losing the respect of those around her because of her attitude. If not for her beauty and the pull he felt toward her, Tobias wouldn't have anything to do with her either. Since discovering the reason behind her anger earlier that day, Tobias filled himself with determination to push past the hurt that caused her fury toward those around her.

Lying in the cavity of the second snow angel, Tobias looked up into the clear sky. Grateful the snow had abated, he gazed up at the twinkling stars, his breath crystalizing against the deep blue of the sky as he exhaled. He wished he could share this moment with Priscilla, who was probably tucked away in bed for the night. Warmth enveloped him as his thoughts wandered. He could still feel her in his arms; the warmth of her cheek pressing against his chest had seeped through the fabric of his shirt. He was certain she hadn't been aware that he'd kissed her on her forehead. If she had, she most likely would have yelled at him for that too. While any other *mann* would probably run from Priscilla, Tobias saw gaining her love as a challenge. He felt he understood her, whereas none other would dare look past her ferocity.

Priscilla tossed around, trying to find warmth beneath the quilts piled onto her bed. She wrapped herself up in them, but nothing brought relief from the cold that invaded the small *haus* where she and her *mamm* lived. Her *daed* had always tended the fire at night, keeping the *haus* toasty warm in winter, but with him gone, the task became her responsibility. She was too cold to get up, but it was her duty to care for her *mamm* in her *daed's* absence. She reluctantly pushed back the quilts, grabbing her knitted shawl and wrapping it about her shoulders.

As she entered the sitting room, her heart sank when she realized she'd forgotten to gather enough wood for the night. Her cousin, Gabriel, had cut and stacked enough wood to get them through the winter, but every wedge was stacked against the barn. She shivered at the thought of having to go out into the cold night to fetch firewood, but if she didn't, the *haus* would be unbearably cold within a couple of hours. It was already cold enough in the *haus* to make her shiver, and she knew that waiting was too much of a risk. Pulling on her boots and heavy wool coat, Priscilla forced herself out into the frigid night air.

The sound of a closing door startled Tobias. He sprang up from the ground like a jackrabbit and ducked behind a large oak tree. He watched as Priscilla walked out toward the side of the barn. What was she doing outside so late? He moved slowly across the yard until he could see her pushing at the layer of snow that had accumulated over the top of the wood pile. She was obviously getting ready to gather wood for the *haus,* and he couldn't stand by and watch her struggle.

He advanced toward her cautiously, certain that she had heard him approach. "Let me help you with that," he said as he took a step closer.

Priscilla jumped back and screamed, putting a hand to her chest to calm her racing heart. "What are you doing out here this time of night?"

How was he going to answer her without giving away his surprise? He picked up a few pieces of cut wood, hoping to buy himself some time to think of a reasonable explanation that wouldn't be a lie.

"I—uh came out here to—uh check on you," he stammered.

It was partially true—at least in theory.

They walked up toward the *haus,* Tobias's arms weighed down with a stack of wood. Priscilla stopped in her tracks when they faced the snow angels that lay just beyond the porch. She felt as frozen as the blanket of snow that covered the yard. Had Tobias made the snow angels, or had she been visited by real angels?

Chapter Four

"I know you made the snow angels," Priscilla told Tobias, trying to hide her disappointment.

"I didn't do it to upset you," he admitted, worried by the misty-eyed beauty beside him.

She seemed to be in shock.

Tobias juggled the three wedges of firewood in his other arm and slipped his free hand into Priscilla's. Her hand clamped onto his, but she remained motionless. It took all his willpower not to drop the stack of wood and pull her into his arms. He wanted to comfort her and ease her pain, but he feared she would only reject him. He'd seen the way she was vying for his *bruder's* attention when they were skating. Tobias knew better than to hope that Priscilla would be interested in him. All the women liked Jesse; he was older and more confident. Tobias had always felt like the awkward younger *bruder* who was always stuck in Jesse's shadow.

Priscilla gasped, letting go of his hand as if she suddenly realized what she was doing. She rushed toward the door, leaving Tobias stunned for a moment. He hurried to catch up to her, shifting the heavy firewood in his arms. Following her into the sitting room after stomping the snow off his boots, Tobias placed all three wedges onto the pile of embers in the fireplace. Priscilla handed him the poker so he could stir them up. The moist firewood popped and sizzled as it slowly caught fire.

Once the fire was well underway, Tobias continued to stir the coals mindlessly. The only sound between them was the crackling and popping of the fire. Heat poured into the small room, and Priscilla stood close to him, her bare hands extended toward the fire. She pulled off her knitted hat and her auburn hair tumbled over her shoulders. The amber glow of the fire brought out the red in her hair and illuminated her porcelain skin. She looked at him with green eyes that bore into him. He didn't want to leave her. He wanted to weave his fingers through her hair and kiss her.

"*Danki,*" she whispered through rosebud lips.

Unable to resist her any longer, Tobias cupped his hands around Priscilla's face and drew her to him until their lips touched. He closed his eyes against the sweetness of her kiss, lingering over her lips. Her breath warmed his neck as he pulled her closer to him. He felt her lips lightly kiss his temple as he held her close, fearing if he let her go the spell between them would be broken. Was he dreaming this? He moved his head to the side and found her lips again, this time with a hunger that matched her own.

"I could kiss you forever," he whispered between kisses.

Priscilla tensed. What was she doing? She'd let her guard down, and she couldn't risk her heart getting broken. Kissing Tobias was *wunderbaar gut,* but Amish *menner* died too easily. She couldn't risk losing another *mann* she loved without losing her mind. As tough as it was to do, she pulled away from him. Her throat constricted, and tears welled up in her eyes. She swallowed hard, trying to push down her emotions. She couldn't even look at him.

Tobias cleared his throat. "I—uh, I'll go get some more firewood."

Before she could object, he was out the door. He would likely expect to court her now, but she couldn't allow it. After seeing what her *mamm* had been through since her *daed* and *bruder* had passed away, Priscilla could never allow herself to marry and risk losing a husband and *kinner.* Her *mamm* had not recovered since the funeral, and Priscilla feared she would never be the same. If she opened her heart to Tobias, Priscilla knew she wouldn't be able to bear losing him. She told herself it was better to end things between them now before she'd vested too much of her heart. The thought of it hurt too much already, but she knew if she prolonged their relationship it would hurt more later. It was best to end it now before it was too late.

Tobias returned with an armful of firewood, set it beside the hearth, and quickly exited the room. Priscilla had kept her gaze on the fire, avoiding eye-contact with him when he'd paused to look at her. When he returned with another armful of wood, Priscilla steeled herself against his charm. No matter how much she wanted to be in his arms again, or how much she'd enjoyed the feel of his mouth on hers, it had to end.

After unloading a second armful of wood, Tobias took a step toward her. Priscilla stepped back, unable to look him in the eye. She feared if she did she would surely burst into uncontrollable sobs.

He reached up and brushed her cheek with the back of his hand but she shied away.

"*Danki* for bringing in the firewood, but it's very late. *Guten nacht.*"

Tobias advanced toward her, dipping his head to kiss her, but she turned her face.

"*Guten nacht,* Tobias," she whispered.

Tobias pursed his lips, feeling confused and rejected. "*Jah, guten nacht.*"

Priscilla regretted every step he took toward the door. She wanted to call out to him, but she couldn't find her voice. Her arms ached for him, her heart feeling as if it was broken like shards of glass. She'd hurt him; she'd seen his blue eyes cloud over with agony. He loved her; she could see it in his eyes. If only she was brave enough to allow herself to love him back. He lumbered across the hardwood floors, his steps hesitant. She missed him before he even walked out the door.

What had she done?

Chapter Five

"Why didn't you tell me you wanted to court Jesse? How could you kiss me like that if you didn't like me?"

Priscilla couldn't face Tobias, who was obviously more hurt than the night before when she'd practically kicked him out of her *haus*. How could she admit to him that going after his *bruder* was a defense against her heart to keep it from breaking? She didn't like Jesse; she was in *lieb* with Tobias, but fear wouldn't let her admit it. Jesse was unattainable, and therefore *safe* for her heart. If she could convince herself that Tobias wasn't for her, then perhaps the sting of his words and the truth wouldn't hurt so much. But now he'd discovered what she'd been up to for the past few days.

"Who I like is none of your business," Priscilla said before she could stop the words from leaving her lips. "But if you must know—I don't like anyone!"

Tobias's expression fell. "That kiss last night meant nothing to you?"

She wanted to tell him it meant everything to her, that she loved him, but her mouth wouldn't form the words. Instead, she jutted out her chin and turned her back on him. She had humiliated herself with her foolishness, and now she didn't know how to undo it.

Tobias wasn't willing to give up on her so easily. There was a reason she was turning a cold shoulder to him, and he didn't believe it had anything to do with Jesse. He could see how much hurt she carried around and how she plainly needed to be loved. He grabbed her hands and twirled her easily on her skates, bringing her with him to the other side of the pond where they could talk without being overheard.

Priscilla tried to pull away from him, but he tucked her arm in the crook of his elbow and let his skates glide swiftly across the ice. It was a perfect day; the sun shone high above them and glistened across the ice. If not for the fact it was almost blinding, she would think it was beautiful. She no longer had the energy to fight Tobias or the pull on her heartstrings. She wanted to tell him the truth, but she couldn't force the words from her throat. She would just have to live with her shame.

Priscilla whirled around. "Can't we just be friends?" she begged.

"Friends?" he practically shrieked. "I can't go back to being just your friend. That kiss meant something to me—even if it meant nothing to you."

Tobias skated away from her, leaving her feeling more humiliated and heartbroken than she ever thought possible.

✳✳✳✳

"You need to work out your differences with *mei bruder,* Tobias," Jesse scolded Priscilla.

She could feel everyone's eyes on her, and she laughed nervously as though Jesse had told her something funny. If it got back to Ruby that Jesse had reprimanded her, she'd suffer even more humiliation.

"Skate with me to the end of the pond so that our conversation won't be overheard by everyone," Priscilla pleaded with him.

He abided by her wishes, taking her hand and placing it in the crook of his arm. Onlookers would conclude that they were a couple skating together, and that was exactly what she wanted everyone to think— especially Tobias. When they reached the other end of the icy pond, Priscilla twirled anxiously while Jesse sat down on the bench and adjusted his skate.

"I can tell that Tobias likes you, and I don't want him getting hurt. If you don't like him, tell him the truth, but don't kiss him and then tease him the way I heard you did."

Priscilla fumed, her face heating with anger. She didn't want to talk about Tobias. It hurt too much.

"I didn't tease him. I changed my mind is all."

Jesse scowled. "That's pretty immature, don't you think? Don't you think you owe him an explanation?"

"It was one kiss! I didn't marry him!"

Priscilla skated in little circles in front of the bench where Jesse sat. If she didn't change the subject, she was going to cry. His words made her angry, and she wondered if others would think the same of her.

"Perhaps while Ruby is recovering from her fall, I can continue your instruction. You still seem a little wobbly on your skates. I'm well aware that was the only reason you let me hold onto you just now when we skated down to this end of the pond."

She desperately needed a distraction, and she didn't care what it was—as long as it kept the ache in her heart for Tobias from pulling her down.

"This isn't going to work, Priscilla," Jesse said impatiently. "I appreciate your offer to help me, but I'd rather skate alone and work on the things Ruby already taught me before…"

"Before you knocked her down and probably crippled her for life," Priscilla barked. "You should be ashamed of yourself for pushing her!"

She hadn't meant to say it, but it just sort of spilled out like word-vomit. It seemed the more she tried to stifle her feelings for Tobias, the more anger rose up in her and spilled out into everything she said.

Jesse finished adjusting his skate and stood up, towering over Priscilla. "That was an accident, and you know it, Priscilla."

Prissy folded her arms and held her ground.

"Tell that to Ruby!"

Why couldn't she just be quiet? She could see how much her mean-spirited words were hurting Jesse. More than that, she was hurting Ruby, and the girl had no idea. But how could she put a stop to her anger?

"Does Ruby blame me for the accident?" Jesse asked timidly.

The corners of her mouth turned up with contempt. "Of course she blames you; she might never skate again!"

Jesse squared his shoulders and pushed past her onto the ice.

Priscilla skated slowly to the other side of the pond, trying desperately to keep her composure. She could not lose control in front of everyone in the youth group, no matter how much she was hurting. All she knew was that if she didn't leave now, she was going to fall apart, and that was just not acceptable.

Chapter Six

Priscilla found herself covered in snow as she formed the snow angel in Tobias's yard. It was dusk, and he would be returning soon from being with his friends. She had to do something to make up for the mess she'd caused everyone, and she would start with Tobias. She was confused about what she wanted, and though trying to convince Ruby that she was attending the skate party with Jesse was one of her biggest lies, the truth was more difficult to accept. She'd messed things up between herself and Tobias. By pushing him away and making everyone think she liked Jesse, she'd made a fool of herself and hurt everyone in her path—including herself.

As her arms and legs formed the angel, she felt a peace wash over her. Was this how it felt to have *Gott* forgive you? Tears welled up in her eyes, and she began to pray out loud, raising her voice toward Heaven.

"Gott, forgive me for the mess I've made of everything. I've hurt so many with my lies. Heal the hurt and the emptiness I feel over losing mei daed and mei bruder. I miss them so much. Take away the fear in my heart over loving Tobias. I do love him, Gott, but I'm afraid if I do, then he will leave me the way mei daed and bruder did. Please put forgiveness in the hearts of those I've hurt—especially Ruby and Tobias."

Priscilla stood up slowly, surveying the perfect snow angel. Would it be enough to let Tobias know how she felt? She knew she would have to apologize to him—and to Ruby, but she prayed the snow angel would be a start. He'd made one for her, and she hoped that hers would be viewed as a peace offering and a symbol of her true feelings for him.

Tears welled up in Tobias's throat at Priscilla's confession. But more than that, she loved him—he'd heard it with his own ears! He stood behind the edge of the *haus* unable to bring himself to disturb her. If she knew he'd overheard her prayer, she might never trust him. He didn't mean to hear it, but he also couldn't help but listen when he'd heard his name mentioned. To top it off, she'd made him a snow angel. It was a peace offering he knew, but how would he thank her for it without letting her know he'd overheard her and seen her in his yard? Then it came to him; he knew just how to break through to her, and hopefully win back her heart in the process.

✳✳✳✳

Priscilla entered her *onkel's* small *haus* that she shared with her *mamm*. It was the same *haus* they'd spent every summer when she was growing up, but now they had come to live in it permanently. Though her *daed* and *bruder* were no longer here with them, there were many memories in this small *haus*. Memories of *familye* picnics and community barn-raisings and work-frolics. Her *daed* and older *bruder* had been like heroes to her. She had always admired their hard work, but more than that, the safety she'd felt when they were around. Laughter no longer filled this small *haus,* and Priscilla had never felt more vulnerable.

Her *mamm* sat at the small table in the kitchen when she entered the room. The woman didn't look up from her sewing; she didn't even hesitate a single stitch. Priscilla sat down across from her and picked up one of the dolls they made for one of the local stores and began to stitch the hem of her apron. The income from the doll sales, coupled with the knitted items they made, brought in enough revenue to keep food on their table without having to depend too much on their *familye*. Still, Priscilla admittedly didn't enjoy the hard work it took to keep them afloat.

"The Christmas Skate for the youth is on Saturday," she said to her *mamm*.

Priscilla knew her *mamm* heard every word she said to her, but she never said much if anything at all.

They used to talk and laugh; they cooked together while her *mamm* would tell her funny stories from her childhood. But now, they barely spoke, and it hurt Priscilla more than she dared admit.

"I won't be out late. I'll probably go with *mei* cousins."

No response.

"Everyone has to bring a lantern so we can see to skate. I can take the extra one from the barn if that's alright."

Still nothing.

Priscilla finished the apron hem and picked up a pair of shears to cut the black fabric for the doll bonnet. The swish of the scissors echoed in the quiet room and Priscilla wondered if her *mamm* had gone mad. She couldn't take the silence between them any longer. She hadn't only lost her *daed* and *bruder* the day of the accident, she'd lost her *mamm* too.

Slamming down the scissors on the table, Priscilla stood abruptly, her chair falling on its side with a loud crash. Her *mamm* looked up from her task, shock on her face.

"It's about time I get a reaction out of you!"

Chapter Seven

"Is something wrong, Prissy?"

Priscilla knew she had to calm down before she said something hurtful to her *mamm*. She'd been saying a lot of hurtful things to people lately, and she didn't want to add her *mamm* to the long list of people she needed to apologize to. She'd been taught to respect her elders, and she wouldn't sway from that upbringing now, no matter how upset she was.

"I miss the way we used to talk when we worked. I miss the sound of *familye.*"

Her *mamm* looked up from the sewing in her hands, suddenly realizing she hadn't spoken more than a handful of words to her *dochder* in months—not since the accident.

"I miss it too, Prissy."

Priscilla reached across the table and pulled her *mamm's* hands into hers. "I know things are not the same as they were before, but we are still a *familye*. I may be grown up, but I'll always be your *dochder.*"

Tears formed in her *mamm's* tired eyes. Prissy recognized the despair she saw in her *mamm's* expression; it was the same deep sorrow she saw in her own reflection every day.

"I don't know how to fix this," her *mamm* whispered.

Priscilla's heart clenched. "I don't need you to fix it, but I do need you to help me put this behind us. We can't change the past, but we can change how we spend the rest of our days on this earth. I don't want to mourn for the rest of my life; I want to be happy again. They wouldn't want us to live out our days with a cloud of doom in our hearts; they would want us to live on and be happy again."

Tears pooled in her *mamm's* eyes, threatening to spill out. Neither of them moved more than a shallow breath for several minutes. Priscilla felt the shifting of *Gott's* warmth pass between them just as surely as she felt the melancholy lift from her heart. Hope rekindled in her heart, rejuvenating her spirit. For the first time in nearly a year, Priscilla felt *normal.* The dark cloud of mourning no longer hovered over her thoughts, and though she would always miss her *daed* and *bruder,* she knew she would be with them again in Heaven someday.

"Do you feel that, *Mamm*?" she was almost too afraid to ask.

Smiling, her *mamm* nodded. "The peace of *Gott.* I feel it!"

"It's a Christmas miracle!"

"I pray it is so," her *mamm* said softly.

Priscilla flung her arms around her *mamm*. "It is for sure and for certain."

They both laughed for the first time since the accident. It felt liberating to be able to laugh; it had been long overdue.

Priscilla crossed to the stove and warmed up some milk for hot cocoa. Her *mamm* picked up her sewing again.

"Do you plan on attending the Christmas Skate Party on Saturday?"

Priscilla froze. She was too embarrassed to confide in her *mamm* about the way she'd been acting—especially since her bad behavior was the very reason she would *not* be attending the Christmas Skate.

"Is something wrong, Prissy? Don't tell me no one offered to escort you."

"Nee," she admitted. "I was hoping to go with Tobias Fisher, but I messed up my chances of that happening."

Priscilla slumped back into her chair at the table and tucked her fists under her chin. She felt discouragement settle in her all over again. She had made a big mess of things, and she wasn't certain how she was going to fix it.

"Anything I can help with, Prissy?"

Tears welled up in her eyes. "I've made such a mess of things, *mamm*. I don't think anyone can fix it. Ruby is mad at me, and so is Tobias. I've lied to everyone. I didn't mean to, *mamm.* I've been so angry with *Gott* for taking away *mei familye* that I've taken it out on everyone around me—even you. I'm so sorry, *mamm.*"

The woman looked up from her sewing. "I've always found that honesty is best in these situations. Remember that an apology can go a long way." She smiled gently.

"Danki, Mamm. I guess I have a lot of apologies to make."

Her *mamm* nodded.

Priscilla stepped over to the stove and poured the steaming milk into two cups. She silently spooned in the cocoa while her thoughts reeled.

"What if Tobias won't accept my apology?"

Her *mamm* grasped her cup of cocoa. "All you can do it try. If you don't take a chance, you won't know what *Gott* has in store for you. If Tobias cares for you, he will listen. Give him a chance to understand your dilemma by letting him know the truth."

Priscilla sipped her hot beverage, remembering the kiss she and Tobias shared. It was the most *wunderbaar* feeling ever. She knew without a doubt that she loved him, but she feared her lies may have stifled any feelings he may have returned. But she also knew her *mamm* was usually right about most things, and so she tried not to fret.

"I will tell him later today when I see him at Goose Pond. But what about poor Ruby? She was stuck at home with her sprained ankle while I was trying my best to sabotage her relationship with Jesse for my own selfish reasons."

Her *mamm* smiled lovingly. "You must tell her immediately what really happened. If you don't, you will lose your nerve. Be certain to apologize—those words of regret go a long way. She will see your true heart, and so will Tobias. But it seems to me you owe an apology to Jesse as well."

"Jah," Priscilla admitted. "I've really made a mess of things. Please pray for me to have the courage to make it right with everyone before the skate party."

Her *mamm* nodded with a smile that Priscilla hoped would remain in her heart.

Chapter Eight

Tobias hurried through his morning chores so he could go to the pond to prepare for the surprise he had in mind for Priscilla. He was thankful it wasn't snowing, and when the youth gathered around the pond in a few hours for the day, Priscilla would be among them and would see what he had planned for her. He knew it would be his only chance to ask her to accompany him to the Christmas Skate tomorrow night, and he hoped his efforts would smooth things over with her enough to get her to accept his invitation.

"Why are you in such a hurry this morning?" Jesse asked.

Tobias struggled with his thoughts momentarily, wondering if he should share his plans with his older *bruder*. He *had* to tell someone, feeling he would burst if he didn't reveal his love for Priscilla. He worried his announcement would welcome some opposition from Jesse, but he wasn't certain he cared what his *bruder* thought. It was how he felt about her, and there was nothing he could do to stop the love he had in his heart. But that didn't stop him from fearing judgment from Jesse.

"I have something I need to do for someone."

Jesse slapped Tobias on the shoulder.

"Whatever it is, I'll help you, so you can slow down a bit on these chores."

"*Nee,* this is something I need to do on my own."

Jesse looked at his *bruder* questionably. "We always work together. That is what gets the work done sooner. I don't mind helping you."

Tobias raised an eyebrow and rested the handle of the pitchfork under his chin. "Even if it's for Priscilla Miller?"

Jesse immediately stopped pitching fresh hay into the horse stall and leaned against the pitchfork, mirroring Tobias. "Aren't you taking my request to keep an eye on her a little too seriously?"

Tobias shook his head and picked up the shovel to muck out the stall next to the clean one. "I knew you wouldn't understand," he said under his breath.

Jesse leaned over the edge of the horse stall. "I can't understand if you don't give me a chance. Whatever it is, you can tell me, Tobias. Make me understand."

Feeling suddenly very exposed and vulnerable, Tobias shook his head and went about finishing the chore.

Jesse chuckled. "You always were stubborn as a mule, little *bruder.*"

Tobias looked over his shoulder, sneering at Jesse, who was still laughing. "That is exactly why I won't tell you anything."

Jesse's eyes grew wide. "You like her!"

"So what if I do?" Tobias said as he shoveled manure into the wheel barrow.

Jesse shook his head. "When I asked you to keep her away from me and Ruby, I didn't mean for you to take it so seriously. I asked you to keep her occupied, not to fall in love with her!"

"Who said anything about love?" Tobias asked, his face heating up with anger.

"You didn't have to tell me; I can see it in your eyes."

Tobias turned sharply, manure flying off the end of the shovel and landing just short of his *bruder's* boots. "Why is it a problem if I love Priscilla?"

Jesse looked down at the mess his *bruder* was making and snatched the shovel from his hands. "Let me do this. You're too upset to do this right now, and you're making more of mess than you're cleaning up."

Tobias stood aside and let Jesse take over the dirty work. He was perfectly content to pitch in the fresh hay instead. "Are you going to answer me?"

Jesse paused. "How can I put this nicely? Priscilla isn't exactly the woman I would choose for you. She isn't a very nice person."

Tossing a final pitchfork full of hay into the stall, Tobias dropped the tool on the floor. "That's because you don't know her like I do. She's hurting from the loss of her *daed* and *bruder,* and even though she has taken out her anger on others around her, she has a *gut* heart. Her circumstances don't make her a bad person, just a person who is very much in need of love and understanding, and I intend to give her just that." Tobias stormed off toward the other side of the barn. He would gather the eggs and take them into his *mamm* so he could hurry along breakfast. The sooner he finished with his obligations at home, the sooner he could get to the pond to set up his surprise for the woman he loved.

Jesse put down the shovel and followed Tobias toward the chicken coop that was situated inside the back end of the barn. He couldn't leave things like that between them. Just because he didn't agree with Tobias didn't mean he wouldn't support him if Priscilla was the one he loved. Besides, maybe with someone to love her, Priscilla would be nicer to those around her—especially to Ruby, whom Jesse loved dearly.

Following the sound of disconcerted hens, Jesse found his *bruder* just before he exited the barn with a pail-full of fresh eggs. "I'm sorry I wasn't more supportive when you trusted me with your feelings for Priscilla. I guess I allowed the shock of it to put words in my mouth that shouldn't have come out. I didn't mean to sound like I disapproved. I have faith in your judgment, and if you have faith in her…well, then that is *gut* enough for me."

The look on Tobias's face softened. "*Danki,* that means a lot to me that you are behind me on this. I'm already nervous enough that she will reject my offer to escort her to the Christmas Skate tomorrow night."

Jesse tipped his head to one side, confusion setting in. "Why would she turn you down?"

Tobias looked at him sheepishly. "We got into a bit of an argument."

Jesse chuckled nervously. "I hope it didn't have anything to do with me." He could tell by the look on his *bruder's* face that he'd hit a nerve.

"We had a misunderstanding, but I know now that she doesn't like you—she's actually *in lieb* with *me!*"

Jesse's face flushed. "That's a relief, but why would she turn you down if she is in love with you?"

"We haven't exactly settled our differences yet, but she left a peace offering for me, and I intend to do the same for her."

Tobias hoped his plan would work; it seemed it was his only hope.

Chapter Nine

"You want to do what?" Jesse hollered. "Do you have any idea how many miles it is around this pond? Almost five, that's how many!"

Tobias scoffed at his *bruder*. "I don't intend to go all the way around the pond, just the short end where everyone usually sets their lanterns. This is where we always skated, and I want to be sure she sees it."

Jesse sighed. "Everyone is going to see it. Are you sure this won't embarrass her?"

Tobias scanned the area; there was no one in sight. "No one will know that they are for Priscilla. Only she and I will know—and you, of course, but I know you won't say anything." He looked to Jesse for reassurance that his secret was safe with him.

"I'm *not* going to tell anyone that I helped you with this. I certainly pray that no one shows up here early and catches us!"

"Me too," Tobias agreed. "I figured if I start at the far end and you start here, we should have this done in less than thirty minutes."

Jesse shook his head. "It's going to take longer than that!"

"Nee, Jesse, each one only takes about a minute. You just drop, swish, get up, and do the next one!"

Jesse shook his head as he began to walk to the far end of the pond. It was a *gut* thing they were only making the snow angels along the short end of the oblong-shaped pond. By the time they finished with this much they would both be frozen to the bone. As he trudged through the deep snow to the other side, he called behind him. "I should have found out what you were up to before I volunteered to help you!"

Laughter echoed in the shelter of the trees that surrounded the pond. Blackbirds flapped from the tree branches as though they had been spooked by the sudden noise. They soared overhead as if to mock them, and Jesse felt foolish for what he was about to do for his *bruder* and Priscilla. He supposed he would do the same for Ruby if the situation were reversed.

Tobias dropped to the snow to make the first angel. His hope was that Priscilla would see his effort in a romantic light and accept his offer to escort her to the Christmas party tomorrow. If she accepted, and they had as *gut* a time as he suspected they would, then he would ask to begin to court her.

✳✳✳✳

Priscilla readied herself to attend the last skate practice before the party tomorrow. She wasn't certain she even wanted to go since she didn't want to be embarrassed by not having an escort, but today, she had apologies to give and she felt newness in her spirit. Her plan was to talk to Ruby, Jesse, and Tobias all together so she wouldn't have to repeat herself or drag out the pain of it any longer than she had to. She hadn't even brought her skates with her, as she did not intend to spend any time on the ice. She was early, but she wanted to be the first to arrive so she could get everyone together for a quick chat in order that she could be gone before the youth arrived and started pairing off. She was filled with much remorse over what had transpired over the past several days, but it would soon be over—she hoped.

Priscilla stepped through the deep snow carefully so as not to get her boots too wet, for she had to walk all the way back home and didn't want to freeze on the way. She needed new boots this year but had declined, telling her *mamm* she could make it through another winter with them. If truth be told, she didn't want to burden the woman with another expense they didn't need when they were still trying to get on their feet since the accident. There were a lot of things she had endured for the sake of her *mamm*, and hadn't wanted to cause her to ask her *onkel* for assistance. It was bad enough they were residing in his *haus,* but her *mamm* could not afford the luxuries they used to be able to when her *daed* was working full time to support their *familye.*

As she neared the pond, Priscilla thought she saw Jesse. As she drew nearer, she could see that Tobias was there too.

They were making snow angels!

Priscilla ducked behind a tree and watched the two of them as they continued to drop the ground and swish their arms and legs into an arc to form the angels. Was Tobias mocking her? Why was he having Jesse help him? It angered her that they should put the snow angels out in the open where all the youth would see them when they arrived at the pond for the afternoon skate practice. She felt her heart thump as she watched the two of them. They continued until they met up in the middle of the pond where they stood back to survey their work.

After a few minutes, Tobias and Jesse threw their heads back in laughter. Hurt rose up in Priscilla, and tears threatened to spill from her. She swallowed down the tightness in her throat, determined not to cry over someone who was obviously not crying over her. How would she ever be able to face them again after knowing they were laughing at her?

Unable to control the sobs that pushed their way up through her throat, Priscilla cupped her mitten-clad hand over her mouth and turned from the tree. Fear pricked her like icy water running through her veins. Moving as quickly as she could through the deep snow, she held her hand closely over her mouth to stifle the sobs.

It was too late.

Tobias had spotted Priscilla from the corner of his eye. He took off in her direction calling after her. She quickened her steps and did not look back.

Chapter Ten

"Prissy, wait," Tobias called after her.

Priscilla whipped her head around, red-rimmed eyes filled with tears glared at him.

"Don't call me Prissy!"

Tobias caught up to her, his heart breaking at the sight of her. He wanted to pull her into his arms and soothe away her pain with kisses, but it was apparent she was upset, and he aimed to find out why.

"You interrupted my surprise for you."

"All I saw was you and your brother mocking me! I confided in you about something very painful in my life, and you used it to make fun of me. Not only have you humiliated me, now your *bruder* knows my personal business. It's apparent how much he despises me, but I suppose you agree with him."

Tobias felt his heart clench behind his ribcage. The love he felt for her overwhelmed him. "You don't understand, Prissy. He was helping me make the snow angels as a surprise for you. Jesse doesn't despise you."

"He does because of the lies I told to Ruby. I deserve every bit of contempt he shows me."

She sobbed harder.

Tobias couldn't stand to see her in so much pain, but he resisted the urge to hold her until they had settled things between them. If she truly loved him as much as he loved her, then he couldn't risk upsetting her more. "Jesse doesn't wish to show you contempt."

Priscilla found it hard to resist the smiling blue eyes that gazed upon her, but she had to protect her heart from breaking further. "I saw the two of you laughing. I don't like being made fun of."

Clenching his hands behind his back to keep from pulling her into his arms, Tobias fought the urge. He wanted to kiss her like his life depended on it, but he feared scaring her off. "We weren't making fun of you. We—I would never make fun of you."

Priscilla swiped at a tear that fell unchecked.

"Please leave me alone. This will never work between us. I'm sorry I lied to you, but I can't keep hoping for something between us that can never be."

"If you make me leave, I'm certain my heart will break."

"But I can't…"

"I know what you're afraid of, Prissy. If you make me leave, then you will still be losing another *mann* in your life."

Priscilla stiffened. "I'm aware that your *bruder* doesn't like me!"

Tobias closed the space between them. "He may not like you for himself, but he likes you just fine for *me*."

He wiped away a tear, allowing his fingers to sweep lovingly across her cheek. She sniffled and smiled, and he couldn't resist smiling back at her.

"I don't know if I can do this," she confessed.

Tobias held her close. "How could you turn me away when you know how much it hurts to lose someone you love? Please don't do that to me."

"I don't want to hurt you, but I don't want to get hurt either." She couldn't look him in the eye.

The tension between them twisted like a thick rope, snagging at their ankles. That cord was so taught it ensnared them in their own trap. There was no escaping the love between them, and there was no denying what was destined to be.

Before she realized what was happening, Tobias pressed his lips to hers. Priscilla could not hold back her love from him. She deepened the kiss, allowing her heart to open to the possibilities that lay before them.

Tobias pulled away gently and gazed upon her as he held steadfast, unwilling to let her go. "If it be *Gotte's Wille,* I will be with you until death parts us."

Her eyes clouded over. "That's what I'm afraid of."

He kissed her softly on the forehead. "Let's not worry about what our future holds. Let *Gott* be in control of that. Why don't we take it one day at a time? Say, starting with the Christmas Skate tomorrow? Will you allow me to escort you to the party?"

Priscilla let out a noise that came out half-cry, half-giggle. "*Jah,* I'd love to have you escort me."

Tobias lifted her and twirled her, and then placed a kiss on her lips. "You have made me the happiest *mann* ever. I love you."

Priscilla giggled. "I love you too."

She kissed Tobias eagerly, feeling at peace with the decision to take their relationship slowly—for now. She was in love, and she hadn't felt so free in nearly a year since the accident that had changed everything for her. At this moment, she'd never felt more free. As long as she didn't think past tomorrow, she could allow herself to love him—one day at a time.

The End
{Dedicated to my friend, Priscilla, whose Snow Angels watch over her from Heaven.}

The Gingerbread Haus

A Novella

Chapter One

"Condemned?" Eden cried. "How can they tear down my *haus* before I even get a chance to live in it?"

Eden Fisher stood on the dilapidated porch of the *gingerbread haus,* as she'd always referred to it, trying desperately not to cry as she studied the notice on the door. It had been abandoned since she could remember. When she was younger, she would play here with Ruby and a few of the other girls from school. She'd fallen in love with the *haus* as a young girl, around the same time she fell in love with Gabriel Miller, dreaming she would live in it when they married.

Surveying the scrollwork on the porch rails that crumbled from wood-rot, she envisioned it with a fresh coat of paint and a few nails. Despite the snow that drifted over the rotted slats of the porch, she could envision a porch swing overlooking lilac bushes overflowing with blossoms. She could almost smell them when she closed her eyes.

She knew the *haus* and property well after studying it and making plans for it over the years. She knew exactly where her kitchen garden would go, and even which rooms she would use for her *bopplies.* She would paint the kitchen a sunny yellow and the cupboards white. Her pantry would be filled with canned pickles, chow-chow, and applesauce. She would make quilts for the bedrooms and one for the sitting room to use on cold nights. She envisioned snuggling up in front of the fireplace with her husband and sipping hot cocoa. If the city tore down this *haus,* she feared the demolition of her future along with it.

Thoughts of Gabriel forced their way to the front of her mind, causing her to blush. She imagined him sitting on the porch swing with her, sipping lemonade and talking about their future plans for the farm while they watched the sunset. She gazed in the front window at the hardwood floors that were in need of repair and a *gut* scrubbing. The hearth needed cleaning, and most of the bricks had fallen to the floor. She shivered as she watched snow drift down onto the hardwood floor from holes in the roof.

Still, she could envision it with her own *familye* living there. She would make curtains for the cloudy windows that she would keep so clean the sun would always shine through. The front door would boast a wreath of pine garland and holly berries at Christmas time, while baskets of ferns and fresh flowers would grace the porch in the summer.

It was a dream she'd been dreaming for a long time, but this would be the last time she would lay eyes on this *haus*. She would always think about the *gingerbread haus* with fond memories, but now all she could see were her dreams being shattered with one word—*Condemned.*

Gabriel Miller rode into town as fast as his mare would take him, the *Notice of Condemnation* tucked away in his pocket. It broke his heart to see Eden crying on the porch of *her gingerbread haus* when he'd passed by earlier after skating at Goose Pond. He hadn't the nerve to disturb her, despite the fact he wanted more than anything to comfort her and kiss away her tears.

Gabriel had been one of the first to tease Eden when they were younger after she'd begun to call the abandoned place the *gingerbread haus*. Truth be told, it did resemble a *haus* made of gingerbread—all except for the gumdrops, but he imagined Eden would paint some large rocks the way she'd always said she would, and line the driveway with them. The *haus* had a lot of potential, and he couldn't believe it would be gone if he couldn't do something to save it.

Gabriel and Eden had known each other since they were younger since she was best friends with his *schweschder,* Ruby. Though he'd loved her for years, it wasn't until a few months ago that they'd begun to be social with one another beyond casual friendship.

Somehow when he wasn't paying attention, love for her had found its way into his heart. They'd been talking to each other at every social function for only a short while, but he'd always known that she was the one he wanted to marry, and he'd hoped they would someday live in her dream home—the *gingerbread haus.*

After calling the number on the notice from the phone shack, Gabriel headed straight into Goshen to meet with the *mann* who he hoped would change the course of his future. If it was within his power to save the *haus,* he would do whatever it took so that he and Eden could someday marry and live there the way he'd imagined they would. He'd been saving for several years to buy the *haus* that bordered his *daed's* farm, and he'd always thought he would have more time. Time was now running out, and he prayed the entire trip that he would have enough to cover whatever the asking price was for the *haus.*

Gabriel felt tightness in his chest as he entered the downtown office. "I'm here to speak with Mr. Winters," he told the woman at the desk.

She picked up a phone and announced his arrival, and then asked him to take a seat in the waiting area. He felt out of place as he sat down in the fancy waiting room of the contractor's office. Copies of *Golf Digest* fanned the table in front of him, and he was tempted to pick one up but decided against it. He fingered the brim of his hat that rested on his lap as he nervously counted the tiles in the floor at his feet.

"You must be Mr. Miller."

The voice startled Gabriel as he stood to meet a stout *mann* in his forties wearing a denim shirt and dark blue slacks.

He extended a hand to Gabriel. "I'm George Winters. Come into my office."

He led Gabriel to an even fancier office behind a set of double doors. He sat in the leather chair offered him while he admired the built-in book shelves that lined the wall behind the L-shaped mahogany desk. Sitting down in the leather chair across Gabriel, George paused, as if studying him.

"What interest do you have my house?"

Gabriel cleared his throat and lifted his gaze to meet George's. "I'd like to save the *haus* from being condemned, Mr. Winters."

George stood from his chair and sat on the corner of his desk, one leg firmly planted on the woven rug that covered the tile floor. "I acquired that little house from a relative I didn't know I had. It was part of my father's estate. I've tried unsuccessfully to sell it for years, but because most of the Amish farmers in the area own the land adjacent to the property, no one seems to want it. The lot is so small and the house is in such bad shape, the city has set it for demolition. It doesn't matter to me because I figured I could at least park some of my equipment there. I'm not in the business of fixing houses; I'm a builder, and we build neighborhoods. I didn't have time to mess with that house. It's a lost cause in my opinion."

Gabriel didn't want to see bulldozers parked in the lot that adjoined his *familye's* acreage. "I think I can fix it, so I would like to buy it."

George chuckled. "You can't be serious, Son. That house is beyond repair, and the land is not worth anything. I didn't think it was worth putting in the money to fix it."

It meant the world to Eden, and a future with her to Gabriel, but he didn't think Mr. Winters would care to hear that. "I can fix the *haus.*"

"I'll tell you what," George began. "I'll sign over the deed to the house to you for consideration of one hundred dollars, but you will have to make all the repairs before the end of the month, or the city *will* demolish it."

Gabriel swallowed hard. That was only a few weeks away. Then he thought about the price and couldn't believe his luck. "I will bring you the money tomorrow morning."

The two shook hands, and Gabriel walked out of his office feeling like his future had just begun.

Chapter Two

Eden arrived at Ruby's *haus,* disappointed that Gabriel was nowhere to be found. She'd barely seen him over the last few days, and was beginning to think she'd imagined his feelings for her over the past few weeks. She was hoping for an invite to the Christmas Skate Party so she would know that they were officially courting, but every day that he didn't ask her brought them closer to the date she feared they would never have.

Her own *bruders* were constantly running off, stating they had somewhere to be, but Eden had no idea what they could all be up to. Perhaps they were making Christmas gifts they didn't want the surprise being spoiled for. All she and Ruby knew was that they were all three being very secretive lately. Eden was happy for the distraction of the work frolic to keep her busy today. It was the Miller's turn to host the Sunday service at their *haus* tomorrow, so Eden had offered to help scrub floors and make food for preparation of the day. Prissy had selfishly opted to stay home.

Happy for a day free of Prissy, Eden eagerly walked into the kitchen, where Ruby and Prissy's *mamm* were already hard at work. There was nothing like a *gut* work frolic to keep her mind off things, and Eden was eager to get started. Knowing she would otherwise spend the day consumed with melancholy over the *gingerbread haus,* she knew hard work was just what she needed to keep her heart from breaking.

Relieved to see Eden walk through the door, Ruby's *Aenti* Beth slowly rose from the floor and stretched the kinks out of her back before handing over her scrub brush.

"I will let you two youngsters finish this floor while I start on the baking. I'm getting too old to be down on that floor scrubbing—it hurts my knees."

Eden smiled at the woman before dunking her brush into the galvanized pail of soapy water and helping her friend with the chore.

"Jesse and Tobias took off as soon as they finished the morning chores again this morning," Eden said, hoping to learn of Gabriel's whereabouts.

Ruby brushed back her hair into her work scarf. "Gabe is gone too. He warned me that if I tried to follow him it would ruin the surprise."

"I kind of thought they were doing something that had to do with Christmas," Eden said. "You aren't even tempted to see what they're up to then?"

Ruby giggled. "Of course I'm tempted, but I have no idea where they've been going. I'm very curious about it."

"Me too," Eden admitted. "But right now I have too many other things on my mind."

Ruby looked at her knowingly. "Try not to think about it. *Gott* has a plan for you and *mei bruder,* and it might not include the *gingerbread haus.*"

Eden blushed. "Am I that obvious?"

Ruby giggled. "*Jah.*"

"No more than you are with *mei bruder,* Jesse!"

Ruby's smile turned to a frown. "If my cousin, Prissy, has anything to do with it, *she* will be marrying Jesse."

Eden rested on her haunches after tossing her scrub brush into the pail. "Jesse doesn't like her!"

"She certainly thinks he does!"

Eden rolled her eyes. "Don't you worry; Jesse likes you—not Prissy."

Ruby frowned. "I pray that you are right. I know Gabriel has liked you for a long time. I've noticed it more in the way he looks at you when you're here and he's around."

Eden repressed the urge to squeal with delight.

"Really? I've had a tough time reading his face, but I did catch him looking at me with dreamy eyes when we skated yesterday."

The both giggled.

"Has Jesse asked you to the Christmas Skate yet?"

"Nee," Ruby answered. "He hasn't mentioned it, but he was watching me skate yesterday. Perhaps he's waiting until he can skate a little better before he asks me; he needs a lot of practice."

"Mei bruder isn't the most coordinated on a pair of skates." Eden stated.

"What about you? Have you been asked yet?"

"Nee. Gabriel hasn't asked me yet either," Eden admitted sadly. "What if we are wrong about the two of them?"

"Don't think that way, Eden. They will ask; they have to."

"Why do *menner* always think we want to be asked at the last minute? It's bad manners to wait, don't you think so?"

"I'm not sure they think about that," Ruby said.

Eden picked her scrub brush out of the bucket and resumed scrubbing the floor. "I wonder how they would feel if they had to wait for us to ask *them*?"

Ruby giggled. "It would probably upset them more than it does us."

"Jah, menner act like *bopplies* most of the time."

They laughed, and Eden felt as if a burden had lifted from her shoulders. It was nice to have Ruby to keep her grounded in her thinking. She wished that they could someday be *schweschders,* but that would depend on whether or not their *bruders* cooperated with their plans.

After finishing the floors, they dusted and straightened before entering the kitchen to help

Ruby's *aenti* with the baking. Earlier, they had brought in a bushel of apples from the barn so they could make a dozen pies. After washing their hands, they each grabbed a paring knife so they could help peel and cut the apples. It was going to be a long day, but at least it would help keep her mind off her troubles.

Chapter Three

Gabriel loaded the lumber, shingles, and paint into the back of the *familye* buggy, praying it would all fit. He knew he would have to make at least two more trips into town to get supplies, but for now, he hoped this would get him started. The first order of business was to patch the holes in the roof, and fix the sagging porch. He'd also bought a length of rope to tie himself off at the chimney. The pitch of the roof reminded him the most of a gingerbread *haus*. It was steep, and he wouldn't take any chances that he could slip and fall. Earlier, he'd taken his tools and ladder over to the *haus*.

Jesse, Tobias, and several other friends would meet him there in less than an hour, and he planned to get as much done each day as he could. With just over three weeks left before the end of the month when the *haus* was scheduled for demolition, they had their work cut out for them. His intention was to be able to finish before Christmas as a surprise for Eden. He'd been to plenty of barn-raisings where they put up a barn in the span of a few days during warm months, but that takes an entire community. His team consisted of only seven *menner,* and because it was winter, he wasn't certain how the weather would fare the outcome of such an undertaking.

Since Gabriel hadn't yet confessed his feelings for Eden to Jesse, he hoped the subject of why he was fixing the *haus* wouldn't come up. He suspected that Jesse had feelings for his *schweschder,* Ruby, and he knew it would smooth things over more if they just came out with the truth to one another. Unfortunately, that wasn't always the way things were handled in the community.

Courting was kept secret. So as far as he knew, Jesse could already be courting his *schweschder,* and he might not discover it until the Bishop published their wedding. He hoped that his friend would be more respectful of his feelings than that, but he had to admit he hadn't exactly been forthcoming with his feelings for Eden either. He couldn't even be certain that Eden herself knew how he felt about her, but she was about to find out.

Not wanting to appear presumptuous, Gabriel decided not to tell Eden outright about his purchase of the *gingerbread haus.* Instead, he'd come up with an elaborate plan of leaving her clues that would lead up to the final moment when he would reveal his gift to her. A sinking thought still weighed him down; what if she was not interested in him the way he thought she was? The only thing that quieted those thoughts was knowing she wasn't presently courting anyone.

Pulling the key from the pocket of his trousers, Gabriel could not forget the pride he felt when Mr. Winters had placed it in his hand. He had a *haus,* but not just any *haus.* He had Eden's dream *haus,* and he prayed she would agree to live in it one day as his *fraa.* He imagined the first time she would gaze upon his handiwork, and he hoped he would be able to do the place justice. It deserved to be taken care of and loved by the one woman who was able to appreciate it even in its dilapidated state.

He turned the key, anticipation reeling through him. The door had swollen in the dampness, but one push from his shoulder and it creaked open. Snow had drifted in from the roof and covered the wood floor, accumulating under each area that needed patching. It was going to take a lot to get this place repaired in time to avoid demolition. Gabriel whispered a prayer of thanks for the opportunity to save the *haus,* and for the chance to show Eden that he loved her.

Gabriel began to unload the buggy, eager to get started. His friends would be here soon, and he wanted to be ready for them when they arrived. He'd spent most of the previous evening plotting out his time for each repair, and estimated he could finish well ahead of schedule. Even if he didn't finish the inside, if he could get the outside to where it wasn't a safety hazard that warranted demolition, he would be satisfied enough to present it to Eden. Perhaps she would want to help, putting a woman's touch to the *haus* to make it her own.

Gabriel and Jesse tied themselves off at the chimney while the others hoisted the sheets of plywood up to them so they could cover the holes in the roof. After examination, they'd determined that the entire roof didn't need to be replaced the way they'd feared. Happy that it would cost less and take less time to repair the roof, which seemed to be the worse of the damage, Gabriel set to work. Despite the cold wind that permeated his wool coat, he was determined to finish the roof today, even if the others had to leave. He would worry about replacing the insulation and repairing the wallboard in the ceiling tomorrow.

Below them, a few of the others busied themselves shoveling the snow and roof debris from the floors, while another stacked the bricks against the wall to prepare for putting them back into the fireplace. Gabriel had stated he wanted to put them back in place personally, knowing how much that fireplace would mean to him once he was married. He hoped to sit in front of it with Eden someday, and he wanted the memories of fixing it to be his own.

If he had the time, Gabriel would have rather done all the work himself, but even though other hands would make some of the necessary repairs, the *haus* was his alone to give to Eden. Gabriel shivered, trying to keep his footing stable on the steep slant of the roof. What he wouldn't give to be cozied up at that fireplace right now with Eden as his *fraa*.

Gott, bless me with the strength to finish this haus for Eden. Surround me and mei friends with safety as we make the repairs needed to save this haus, and please let us finish in time.

Chapter Four

Eden walked home from Goose Pond feeling more discouraged than ever. Gabriel hadn't been there for the third day in a row, and she was beginning to think he was avoiding her. Had she been too eager the last time they'd been together? They'd skated happily around the pond a few times, but he'd acted nervous and preoccupied. She'd talked on and on about Christmas, dropping hints about the skate party, and he'd barely said a word.

"I wonder where everyone was today," Ruby said.

Eden had forgotten she was walking beside her.

"All the *menner* were gone and I don't have a clue where they were today," Ruby continued. "They've seemed to have disappeared the last few days. I wonder if they will be at the Christmas Singing tomorrow."

"You sound worried."

Ruby shook her head discouragingly. "I know *mei bruder* will be there because he is taking me and Prissy. What about you? I know this is supposed to be your first Singing. Will Jesse and Tobias still escort you?"

Eden smiled. "*Jah,* but I suspect you already know Jesse will be there since I saw you skating with him today."

"We had another skating lesson today, which Prissy interrupted," Ruby complained.

"Does she realize that *mei bruder* doesn't like her? He thinks she acts foolish. He tries to be kind to her, but then she takes it the wrong way and thinks he likes her, but he doesn't."

Ruby scrunched her brow. "Are you certain about that? Prissy keeps bragging to me how Jesse is very interested in her."

Eden cupped her arm in the crook of Ruby's elbow. "I could never be certain. Especially since he hasn't officially asked you to the Christmas party. Has he indicated his intentions to you?"

"*Nee,* but it's been a little tough for him since we have such little time together, and Prissy seems to interrupt just at right time—right when he starts to relax a little and open up to me."

Eden sighed. "Have you asked her to leave the two of you alone? You don't have to be unkind, but maybe you should be firm with her—so she gets the hint."

"She already gets it," Ruby said impatiently. "I think she keeps it up just to annoy me!"

Eden thought about it for a minute. "I probably wouldn't say anything to her *mamm* either. The poor woman is so sad."

"*Jah,* she and Prissy have been through a lot this past year. I suppose that is why I tolerate her as much as I do. I keep hoping that in time she will calm down. She just seems desperate to get married, but I pray I'm wrong about that."

"You think she's throwing herself at Jesse because she needs to fill the gap from the loss of her *daed* and her *bruder?*"

Ruby nodded dramatically. "She denies it, but there doesn't seem to be any other explanation."

"Then don't let her discourage you, Ruby. She's obviously trying to make you mad for some reason. Don't give her one. Ignore her."

That was easier said than done, Ruby knew. It was tough staying positive and believing Jesse had plans for her.

❄❄❄❄

"Why did you speak so harshly with Prissy?" Ruby whispered. "Now she's going to tattle on me to *mei daed* for sure and for certain."

Eden waited until Prissy walked to the other end of the Yoder's barn where the rest of the youth gathered for the Singing. "I'm sorry, Ruby, I would never try to get you into trouble, but someone had to say something to Prissy. She's being rude, and you just let her walk all over you with her words."

Ruby clasped Eden's hand firmly. "I know you meant well, but I think you made her even more angry."

"Why don't we spend the rest of the evening enjoying the Singing and those two *menner* that keep smiling at us!" Eden said.

They both giggled like school girls as they locked their gaze upon Jesse and Gabriel.

Chapter Five

Gabriel stood at the hearth deep in thought. Giving this *haus* to Eden as a gift was a risk he was willing to take. He prayed she would share it with him and agree to someday marry him so the two of them could live here together, but it was still a risk. Jesse had already questioned him about it, asking why he'd purchased it, but he hadn't the courage to admit he was doing it all for love. He dreaded being teased relentlessly by the others, but he knew Jesse would be the most understanding. Perhaps not if he knew it was for his *schweschder,* but Gabriel prayed Jesse would understand and accept his devotion to Eden.

"Dreaming of what your life will be like here with *mei schweschder?"*

Gabriel whipped his head around to see Jesse standing in the doorway. He hadn't even heard him approach. "I—um. What?"

"There is only one person I know that loves this *haus* so much that she calls it the *gingerbread haus*. How long were you going to make me wait before you admitted you bought it with Eden in mind?"

"I'm sorry. I hope you aren't angry with me," Gabriel said. "I was trying to find the right time to tell you."

Jesse cleared his throat. "I tried giving you the opportunity last night at the Singing, but I guess you didn't trust me enough. We've been friends too long for there to be secrets between us."

Gabriel felt awful for not confiding in Jesse.

"I'm sorry. I should have trusted you more."

"Does she know yet?" Jesse asked.

"*Nee,* I was going to surprise her and present it to her for Christmas."

Jesse chuckled. "Don't you think you should have a date with her first before you go buying her a *haus?*"

Gabriel's face heated. "I have a plan—I think. I'm already in this with both feet, but I suppose I should have found out if she was even interested in me before I did all this."

Jesse slapped him on the shoulder. "She's plenty interested. Don't you worry!"

Gabriel smiled confidently. If anyone would know, it would be Jesse. He was grateful that the burden of telling him was over. Now if only it could be that easy to tell Eden.

✳✳✳✳

Eden stood across from Gabriel holding the sack of flour he'd handed to her, wondering *why* he was giving it to her. It's not that she was unhappy to get a gift from him along with the request to court her, but she was curious what the significance of the flour was. She didn't dare ask why he would give such an odd gift and wasn't certain she really cared. He was officially asking to court her, and she was elated her prayers had finally been answered.

"*Jah,*" she said shyly. "I would like it if we courted."

Gabriel kicked at the snow. "May I pick you up tomorrow evening for a sleigh ride?"

"*Jah,*" she whispered.

"I'm sorry I can't stay and skate with you, but I have to meet Jesse and the others at..." Gabriel stopped short of telling her where he was going.

"...The place you've been running off to for over a week now?"

It was a question that deserved an answer, Gabriel knew, but he wasn't ready to reveal his surprise yet. "You will find out soon enough. It's kind of a surprise."

"For me?" Eden practically squealed.

Gabriel patted the sack of flour in her hands. "I will tell you soon. This sack of flour is a small token of what is to come."

What could a sack of flour have to do with a surprise he had for her? Was he going to bake something for her, or perhaps take her to *Das Dutchman Essenhaus* for Christmas dinner?

"Now you have my curiosity up," Eden said excitedly.

She gazed upon the smile that lit up his face. He looked tired, and he was in need of a shave, but she liked the scruff that peppered his well-sculpted jawline. His green eyes sparkled in the sun, greeting her with a smile all their own. Whatever he was up to involved her in some way, and it was a surprise. Could she wait long enough to find out what it was? Did it even matter? Whatever it was would certainly take her mind off the loss of the *gingerbread haus.*

Ah, the *gingerbread haus;* courting Gabriel would definitely take her mind off the demolition. Even though she still held onto romantic notions that they would live there someday as a married couple, it had suddenly lost its importance. She would miss the *gingerbread haus,* but she could make a home anywhere if that was what was meant to be.

"Keep that curiosity at the front of your mind until I'm ready to reveal the rest of this."

Gabriel pulled her free hand into his. It warmed her even through her mittens.

"You have fun skating," he said. "I'll see you tomorrow night at seven o'clock."

Eden smiled. She couldn't wait.

Chapter Six

Light, airy snowflakes swirled about like dust floating near a sunny window. A full moon illuminated the bright white snow that covered the ground, and the sparse cloud cover provided a romantic canopy for the perfect sleigh ride.

Gabriel offered his bare hand to Eden, assisting her into the sleigh where several lap-quilts waited to provide a shelter against the crisp night. Settling in beside her, Gabriel pushed his hand back into his glove, the warmth of Eden's hand still lingering there. With one flick of the reins, the horses moved forward, pulling the sleigh along the thick layer of snow.

Eden savored the enchantment as the sound of sleigh bells permeated the icy air. A light spray of snow kicked up from the horse's hooves and dampened their rosy cheeks, but the romantic ambiance kept them warm. Eden's heart beat in perfect rhythm with the sleigh bells, while she snuggled in close to Gabriel.

He steered the sleigh toward Goose Pond.

"Are we skating tonight?" she asked shyly.

"Nee, I doubt anyone is there tonight. I thought we could go there and talk for a while. I can build a fire to keep us warm if you'd like."

She nodded. It sounded romantic. She felt like she was in a dream—the kind you don't want to wake up from or it will all go away.

Gabriel pulled the team onto the lane that led to the pond. It was deserted just like she'd hoped. She wanted him all to herself without the prying eyes of the rest of the youth as onlookers to their private date. Pulling on the reins, Gabriel pulled the sleigh to a stop just short of the stone fireplace that stood at the far end of the pond.

Reaching under the seat, Gabriel pulled out a small box wrapped in plain, brown paper and tied with raffia, a sprig of pine and holly berries tucked beneath the bow. He handed it Eden. "I almost forgot to give you this."

She took it, admiring the simple, but elegant wrapping. "What is this?"

"It's another clue!"

The very thought of it amused her.

Eden giggled. "Does that mean you want me to guess?"

Gabriel smiled and patted her hand. "Not yet. Open the box…"

Eden pulled at the ends of the raffia and opened the flap of the small box. Inside, she found various spices in glass jars, cinnamon sticks and whole cloves. What did it all mean?

She met his gaze, not realizing he was watching her so closely. Normally that would make her feel self-conscious, but she welcomed the stares from the *mann* she loved.

"I'm beginning to think you want me to bake something for you!" she said with a giggle.

The thought of her cooking for him in the kitchen of the *gingerbread haus* was enough to heat him up without even starting a fire. If he had his way, they would begin their lives together now rather than later. The love he felt for her overpowered that little voice inside that told him he was moving too fast. Jesse had told him he was putting the cart before the horse, but he didn't care. He was eager to get started on his future with Eden. For her, he would wait until she was ready to meet him in the place he'd been moving toward for years. He couldn't remember a time when he hadn't loved her. He only wished he'd made his move to court her sooner, but he supposed it was all in *Gott's* timing. *Gott* was in control and knew what He was doing in their lives, and Gabriel was determined to continue to trust in Him.

Eden set aside the unusual gift and took the hand Gabriel offered her. He pulled one of the quilts from the sleigh and tucked it around her as she sat on the bench opposite from the stone fireplace.

Gabriel took an axe from the back of the sleigh and began to chip away at one of the snow-covered logs to fray the edges so it would ignite quicker. Then he gathered some pine needles from beneath the nearby trees and tossed it all into the belly of the fireplace.

Watching him strike a wooden match against the stones, Eden couldn't help but feel the urge to step in and help when he struggled to get the fire to catch. Instead, she sat back feeling amused at his masculine attitude. She'd never had to worry about tending to fires or getting firewood with three *menner* in the *familye,* but she'd done things enough times to know that he might be fighting a losing battle with the damp wood from the woodpile.

With nothing but smoke coming from the quickly-burning pine needles, Gabriel walked back to the sleigh and gathered a few pieces of wood from the back. He'd come prepared after all. Eden leaned back on the bench feeling very proud of this *mann* that she loved more than she was willing to admit yet.

Within minutes, the fire caught on the dry logs he'd put in, and the two of them enjoyed the crackle of the fire that echoed against the crisp air. Eden held her hands and feet out toward the flames to warm them. She felt Gabriel slip his arm around her and pull her close. She shivered, but it was more nerves that caused the reaction than the cold. He leaned his head onto hers and kissed her temple. It was her first kiss, but did it count? She closed her eyes, wishing he'd kiss her on the lips, but to her disappointment, he didn't.

"Are you warm enough," he whispered at her temple.

She lifted her head from his shoulder and met his gaze. "I'm getting there."

His blue eyes trailed her face, focusing on her lips. Was he about to kiss her? His lips slightly parted, Gabriel leaned into her and placed a soft kiss on her cheek, and then stood up to reposition the logs.

That one doesn't count either, she silently fumed.

Eden stood, holding her hands out toward new flames, pretending she needed to be closer to the fireplace. It was an excuse to be closer to Gabriel, and she hoped it would afford her a better chance of deepening the kiss should he make another attempt. It seemed he took the hint and closed the space between them.

"Let me warm you up," he said as he pulled her into his arms.

Thinking he was finally going to kiss her, he disappointed her by placing a kiss on the top of her head.

That's three kisses, and not one of them count!

By this time, she realized that if she was going to get a *real* kiss from him, she had to take matters into her own hands. Pulling away from him slightly, Eden looked up into his thoughtful green eyes and waited, hoping he would make a move.

Gabriel could see the gentle plea in Eden's blue eyes, but he was hesitant to give in to her. He'd wanted to kiss her for a very long time, but he feared that once he kissed her, he wouldn't want to stop. He wanted to spend the rest of his life kissing her, but what if she didn't feel the same way about him? What if she was just looking for a beau and wasn't yet ready to commit to the one she would someday marry? Should he risk breaking the spell between them by asking her?

Before he realized, she'd tipped up on her toes and met his lips with hers. His mouth responded, capturing her in a deep kiss with all the love behind it that he intended for his *fraa*. There was no turning back now. He would propose to her, but first, he would enjoy the kiss she was so lovingly sharing with him.

Chapter Seven

"Why can't you simply tell Ruby how you really feel?" Eden demanded.

Jesse scooped up another shovel-full of snow and tossed it aside. "It's not as simple as you're making it out to be."

"It is too! Ask her to the Christmas party before someone else does."

"It's more complicated than coming right out and asking her. I was trying to get to know Ruby a little better by skating with her—until I nearly broke her leg by falling on her!"

Eden formed a snowball and tossed it back and forth in her hands as if she intended to throw it at her *bruder*. "You aren't going to accomplish anything by skating with Prissy!"

Jesse leaned against the shovel and eyed the snowball in his *schweschder's* hand. "I told Priscilla I didn't want to skate with her, so you can put the snowball down!"

Eden giggled and tossed it playfully at him.

Jesse looked at the spray of splattered snowball on his shoulder. "I'm going to pretend you didn't do that!"

Eden bent down and scooped up another handful of snow. "I'm going to keep throwing them until you promise me you won't break Ruby's heart."

Jesse was getting a little impatient with her. "I don't have a problem promising you that because I have no intention of breaking her heart. The biggest problem I have is asking her to the Christmas Skate. I tried to go over to see her, but she rejected my visit. Priscilla told me she blames me for the accident. Please tell me her ankle is going to be alright."

Eden couldn't resist tossing the snowball at Jesse. "She will be, but the doctor told her to stay off the ankle for a couple of days. She will be able to skate on it Saturday."

Jesse pulled off his hat and smacked it against his leg to dust off the snow. "I can't wait to ask her until the last minute!"

"I'm afraid you have no other choice."

Jesse sighed. "What if she rejects my offer?"

Eden smiled at her *bruder's* furrowed brow.

"She will say yes. Consider yourself lucky she still likes you even after the accident."

"I *knew* she blamed me!" Jesse said.

Eden shook her head. "*Nee.* She just needs time to heal. Give her that time and ask her when you see her Saturday afternoon when she goes to Goose Pond to test out her ankle before the Christmas party."

"What if she gets another offer before then?"

Eden was almost enjoying watching her *bruder* worry so much over Ruby. She knew it would make his feelings for her stronger, and it was important that her friend get the best from Jesse.

"If she does, she won't accept. She wants *you* to escort her."

Jesse let out a whoop, dropping the shovel and scooping up a handful of snow. "It's payback time!"

Eden squealed, reaching down to grab a fistful of snow and tossed it at her *bruder.* His snowball smacked her in the arm, spraying snow everywhere. She threw hers as hard as she could. It went sailing into the air and knocked his hat off his head. He laughed, falling to the ground in defeat.

"You win!"

Eden dusted the ice and snow off her mittens, smiling over her victory.

"I always do!"

Gabriel pulled the sleigh up to Goose Pond with Eden tucked in the quilts next to him. He'd hurried through his evening chores to make it on time to pick her up. He was tired from a full day of work at the *gingerbread haus,* but he was too eager to see her to cancel their date. He'd spent the entire day replacing glass in the window panes, and having to do the task without gloves had left his fingers a little stiff. Thankfully, he was able to keep the reins slack in his hands since his horses were well-trained. They knew where they were going, and Gabriel was thankful for the sturdy team.

Gabriel hopped out of the sleigh and reached under the seat, pulling out a Mason jar with a raffia bow tied around the neck. He handed it to Eden.

She examined it in the dark. "A jar of molasses?"

"*Jah*. You seem disappointed," he said nervously.

"*Nee*, I'm not disappointed in the least. Just curious what this is all leading up to."

She set the jar on the seat beside her and took Gabriel's hand in assistance. Once her feet were on the ground, he pulled her into his arms and pressed his cold lips to hers with a quick kiss.

"You will have to wait until the surprise is ready."

Eden kissed him again. "Are you making me something?"

He pecked her cheek. "Something like that."

Eden had begun knitting him a scarf, but she had a feeling it would pale in comparison to whatever he was up to. He'd involved the entire community of *menner*, she knew, but she hadn't been able to get any more information than that from her inquiries.

"I'm making something for you too!" she said.

Gabriel picked her up and twirled her around, her feet dangling, but she didn't care because his lips were pressed to hers.

"I can hardly wait," he said excitedly.

He set her down, but she remained in his arms.

"For your gift or mine?" she asked.

"Both!" he said as he picked her up and twirled her again.

Eden had to wonder what it was that had him so excited. Was he going to propose to her already? No, that couldn't be it. It was something he was making, and it was gnawing at her curiosity almost to the point of complete unrest.

Chapter Eight

Gabriel had just finished pounding in the last nail of the final slat of the porch floor when he heard a truck pull up to the back of the *haus*. Once the railings were put in place, the porch would be finished. He stood and made a quick observance of his work. Gabriel and his friends had made a lot of progress in less time than he'd planned on. Thankfully the weather had not slowed them down.

"This looks like a whole new house! I can't believe how much you've gotten done."

Turning around, Gabriel met the approval of Mr. Winters, who stood admiring his efforts to revive the *gingerbread haus.* The look on the *mann's* face gave Gabriel an instant confidence boost. He'd been unsure of his decision to fix up the old *haus,* but the look on Mr. Winter's face said it all. One quick look at his friends around him who continued to work hard, and Gabriel felt a gratefulness that could only come from the strong bonds of a community working together.

Extending a hand to Gabriel, Mr. Winters smiled in awe of the transformation. "I can't believe this is the same house! You've done an amazing job of fixing it up!"

"Danki, Mr. Winters. I'm glad you approve. I pray that it will pass inspection to prevent the demolition."

Mr. Winters pulled an envelope from his jacket pocket and handed it to Gabriel. "I'd say it's fine just the way it is, but I can see you have plenty more you intend to do to the house. It is clear that the house no longer poses a threat of danger to the community. I've signed the deed over to you. I'll make sure the inspector knows they can come out and release the demolition. Good luck, Son."

He shook Gabriel's hand once more before turning to leave.

✳✳✳✳

Gabriel carefully wrapped the bag of gumdrops he'd gotten from Fork's General Store and tied a bow of raffia the way his *mamm* had shown him how to do. It was the final clue to give to Eden before the unveiling of the *gingerbread haus.* He decided he couldn't wait any longer, whether it was finished or not. He was going to wait until Christmas to show her, but he hoped it would give him leverage to ensure he would escort her to the skate party on Saturday. Not that he felt he needed the leverage, but as a woman, she always had the option to turn him down.

Then a terrifying thought entered his mind. What if she turned down his proposal? Was he really ready to propose to her so soon? He'd loved her for what seemed his entire life, and he'd known just as long that he wanted her for his *fraa*. But that didn't stop him from feeling unsure of her answer. After the time they'd spent this past week and the kisses they'd shared, he was confident she was his, but his *daed* had always taught him never to be that sure of anything because *Gott* always had His plans too. Gabriel had prayed about his decisions regarding Eden and the *gingerbread haus* to the point that he was fairly confident that it was also part of *Gott's* plan for the two of them. All he needed was reassurance from Eden to confirm his plans for their future.

After packing clean lap-quilts into the sleigh, Gabriel and the box of gumdrops were ready to meet their fate. Snow fell in wet clumps, and he suddenly wished he'd brought an umbrella for Eden. Was it possible the old black one was in the back? The last thing he wanted was for her to think he was inconsiderate. A lot was dependent on the outcome of this date, and he wanted everything to be perfect. It wasn't an absolute requirement, but Gabriel hoped for the perfect setting to establish his place in Eden's heart once and for all. He'd managed to muster up the courage to be bold enough to ask her, and he prayed she would accept not only his proposal to escort her to the Christmas Skate Party, but eventually his proposal of marriage as well.

Eden opened the old black umbrella and held it over her head as Gabriel shook the reins to set the sleigh in motion. Grateful he'd found the umbrella in the back, he was ready to spend a romantic evening with Eden, and didn't want the wet snow to dampen the mood.

All too soon, the sleigh came to a halt in front of Goose Pond near the fireplace, and Gabriel pulled his arm from around Eden to tie up the reins. Ducking his hand under the seat, he pulled out the box accented with a pine branch and holly neatly tucked beneath the raffia bow and handed it to her. He reveled in the delightful glow that lit up her face at the sight of the gift.

"It's the final clue before your Christmas gift," he said.

Eden let out a squeal when she opened the box. She'd heard rumors that Gabriel and her *bruders* had been busy fixing up the *gingerbread haus,* but she'd been too afraid to let herself hope for such a thing. Unfortunately for Gabriel, the buzz in the community had nearly spoiled his surprise for her, but she wanted to wait for confirmation from him that the rumors were true. The contents of the box had been the last clue to revealing what she already knew, but she would never dream of spoiling it for Gabriel. She would wait for him to tell her himself.

Leaning in, she placed a gentle kiss on his cheek, but he turned, meeting her lips with his. He swept over her mouth with a loving hunger for her, satisfied she was without a doubt devoted to him.

Chapter Nine

Gabriel filled in the cracks between the bricks of the fireplace with mortar. He'd been lucky that none of them had broken when they'd fallen out. There were a few chips here and there, but Gabriel thought they only added character to the hearth. Eden would appreciate that every brick was original to the *haus*. The place was not finished, but it was clean and no longer a danger according to Mr. Winters, and that made Gabriel proud.

When the last brick was put into place, Gabriel stood back to observe his work. He intended on putting pine boughs and candles on the mantle to show it off to Eden when he brought her here tomorrow before the skate party. The night before, they'd shared Gabriel's final gift in front of the outdoor fireplace at Goose Pond, and she'd agreed to allow him to escort her to the party. The gumdrops had tasted sweet, but Eden's kisses had been sweeter.

For now, he had scrollwork to finish on the porch to preserve the *gingerbread* look to the *haus.* He would not be seeing Eden this evening, as he planned on working by lantern light if need-be in order to finish as much of the work as possible before he presented it to her tomorrow afternoon. His friends would only be here a few more hours today, and then they would all leave him to finish on his own.

As far as Gabriel was concerned, he would probably see it as a work-in-progress for a long time, and he knew Eden would also want to add her own touches to the *haus* as well. Whatever condition it was in at the unveiling tomorrow for Eden, he was satisfied it was a huge improvement over the dilapidated state it had been in only a few days before. He prayed that Eden would approve of the work he'd done, as he'd tried his best to duplicate or preserve things just as they were when it had been a new home so long ago. It was a challenge pulling from his memory the way it had looked even when they were young *kinner,* but he supposed everything he'd done was a big improvement over being demolished, and he knew Eden would see it the same way.

✳✳✳✳

Gabriel felt his heart pounding like a woodpecker on a tree. If his heart raced any faster, he feared it would turn into one long beat. He steered his sleigh up to the front of the *gingerbread haus* with Eden snuggled close beside him.

"You keep that scarf around your eyes until I get back. I need to light a few lanterns so you can see the surprise I have for you."

He hadn't planned on bringing her here so late in the afternoon, but he'd wanted to finish the porch rails before she saw the *haus* for the first time, and it had taken him longer than he'd planned on.

"It isn't that dark yet, Gabriel. I'm sure I will be able to see it alright."

"Nee," he cautioned. "I want the lanterns to show it off more—sort of give it the look I imagined."

Eden sat patiently in the sleigh, waiting for him while he lit two lanterns and hung them from either side of the porch near the scrollwork. Then he went inside, lit two lanterns, and placed them on each end of the fireplace mantel, adjusting the pine boughs to fit nicely for a holiday display.

Eden heard the crunch of Gabriel's boots in the snow and felt his gentle hand clasp hers as he assisted her out of the sleigh.

"No peeking," he said, as he walked her up the front walk and stood next to her facing the porch.

When he was satisfied she was in the perfect spot to observe the *haus* in its entirety, he slowly removed the scarf from her eyes.

Eden gasped, smiled, and held her breath for a moment. She was too afraid to hope that what she was seeing was real. She took a cautious step forward, taking in the enchantment of the *gingerbread haus* illuminated by lamplight. Taking a step up, she placed her hand on the rail of the porch, taking in every detail of the white-washed scrollwork that had been duplicated to the exact way it had looked to her as a young girl. The floor of the porch no longer caving in, she walked across the new boards that had been swept clean of snow and led to the front door that boasted a fresh coat of red paint. A pine wreath with bits of holly tucked in the folds decorated the door, inviting her to go inside.

"It's all so *wunderbaar,*" she barely whispered around the lump in her throat.

Gabriel clutched Eden's hand and opened the front door for her. Her face glowed in the lamplight, a smile lighting her face as she set her gaze upon the fireplace. He handed her a lantern and allowed her explore the rest of the *haus* while he started the fire. He could hear her laughing and exclaiming awe over every feature while he arranged the logs just right over the grate and set a match to them. Before she returned, the fire had caught and added an amber glow to the cozy sitting room.

Eden approached Gabriel where he waited for her in front of the fire. She threw herself into his arms and pressed her lips to his. "Did you do this for me?"

He chuckled. "Who else would I do this for? I wanted you to have your *gingerbread haus* this Christmas, but I pray we will *both* be living here *next* Christmas!"

Eden looked into his hopeful green eyes. "Are you asking me to marry you?"

"I've loved you for as long as I can remember, Eden," he said. "I bought the *gingerbread haus* and fixed it up for the only person I would want to live here with. I'd like you to be my *fraa.*"

"*Jah,*" she squealed with delight. "I can't imagine living here with anyone but you either. I love you Gabriel."

Picking Eden up and swinging her around the room of their *gingerbread haus,* Gabriel didn't think he could ever be happier than he was right now.

Chapter Ten

Eden looked out at the lanterns that lined Goose Pond, illuminating her friends as they skated happily together. Ruby was skating with her arm tucked neatly in Jesse's elbow, while Prissy was cozy in the arms of Eden's twin *bruder,* Tobias. When had that happened, and how had she not seen that coming? Eden supposed it was because she had been so busy with Gabriel, she'd missed a lot of things that were happening all around her in the community. Eden couldn't be happier for Ruby and Jesse, and even for Tobias and Prissy. They looked happy, and that was all that mattered. She couldn't wait to hear all about everyone's news, but for now, she was content to enjoy the view from Gabriel's sleigh.

It was almost magical.

"I almost forgot to give you my gift," Eden said as she lifted the small box from beside her and handed it to Gabriel.

He looked at her sheepishly and then tore open the brown wrapping. Lifting the flap of the cardboard box, Gabriel hesitated when he gazed upon the contents. "It's a gingerbread *haus!*"

"*Jah,* it looks like we both had the same gift in mind, but I have to admit, yours is a lot better."

Gabriel disagreed. Eden had truly been the one to bless *him* with the *gingerbread haus,* her love, and so much more. He pulled her into his arms and whispered in her ear, reminding her how much he loved her. He would have never attempted the project if it hadn't been for Eden's love of that old *haus.* Now the *haus* and their future belonged to both of them. They would spend a lifetime of love and happiness together in their *gingerbread haus.*

The End

2012 Winners of the Christmas Cookie Contest
Each winner received an autographed copy of Amish White Christmas, and a gift card!

If you would like to SUBMIT a recipe for future books, or be the first to know the next book I'm writing, PLEASE follow me on Facebook using the link below, to receive automatic updates on all CONTESTS, book GIVEAWAYS and book releases.
http://www.facebook.com/SamanthaBayarr

Amish Gingerbread Men: submitted by Diana Montgomery

3 cups all-purpose flour
½ cup unsalted butter (room temperature)
½ teaspoon salt
½ cup granulated white sugar
¾ teaspoon baking soda
1 large egg
2 teaspoons ground ginger
2/3 cup molasses
1 teaspoon ground cinnamon
¼ teaspoon ground nutmeg
¼ teaspoon ground cloves
(non-stick spray)

Frosting:
2 cups confectioners' sugar, sifted
1 teaspoon pure vanilla extract
½ cup unsalted butter room temperature
1 ½ tablespoons milk or light cream

In large bowl sift together flour, salt, baking soda, and all the spices. In another bowl, using an electric mixer, beat the butter and sugar until fluffy. Add the egg and molasses; beat until well mixed. Gradually add the flour mixture until well mixed.
Divide the dough in half, and wrap with plastic wrap. Refrigerate until firm (at least 2 hours or overnight).
Preheat oven to 350 degrees.
Place rack in center of oven.
Line baking sheets with parchment paper.

On lightly floured surface, roll out the dough to a thickness of ¼ inch. Use gingerbread cutter to cut the cookies out. Put on baking sheet placing about 1 inch apart.
Bake for about 8 – 12 minutes depending on the size of the cookies. Cookies are done when they are firm and the edges are just beginning to brown. Remove the cookies from oven and cool on sheet about a minute then transfer to a wire rack to cool completely. Decorate as desired.

Frosting:
Using an electric mixer on low, beat the butter until smooth and well blended. Add the vanilla extract. Then gradually start adding the sugar, and mix well. Scrape down the sides of the bowl and beaters. Add milk and beat on high speed until frosting is light and fluffy (about 3-4 minutes). Add a little more milk if needed. Tint frosting with food coloring if desired.

Place frosting in pastry bag, fit with deco tip and
decorate the gingerbread men as desired.
Makes about 3 dozen cookies depending on the size of
cookie cutter.

**White Christmas Jubilee Fudge: submitted by
Joan Bolen**
18 ounces white chips
1 can sweetened condensed milk
1 1/2 teaspoon vanilla
pinch salt
1/2 cup green candied cherries chopped
1/2 cup red candied cherries chopped
Directions:
in sauce pan on medium heat, melt chips. Add milk
and stir in vanilla and salt.
Remove from heat and stir in candied cherries.
Pour into lightly greased 8x8 pan.

Refrigerate until firm.
Cut into squares and enjoy.

Easy Cherry Almond Fudge: submitted by Jill Greer

1 bag (12oz) white vanilla baking chips
1 container cherry frosting
½ cup chopped red candied cherries (4oz)
½ cup slivered almonds, toasted
1 teaspoon vanilla
Dash salt

Line 9 inch square pan with foil, spray it with cooking spray. In a large bowl, microwave
baking chips uncovered on high 1 minute to 1 minute 30 seconds. Make sure to stir every 15 seconds, until melted.
Stir frosting into melted chips. Fold in remaining ingredients. Pour and spread into pan. Refrigerate 20 minutes or until set.

Using foil, lift fudge out of pan, remove foil. Cut into
6 rows by 6 rows. Store tightly covered.
Makes 36 candies

Peppermint Stick Cookies: submitted by Jill Greer

¾ cup butter
6 Tablespoons sugar (additional for dipping)
1 egg, separated
1 teaspoon vanilla extract
2 cups sifted all-purpose flour
½ cup crushed peppermint sticks or candies
Chocolate kisses
Preheat oven to 350F.
Put parchment paper on cookie sheets.
Cream butter and 6 tablespoons sugar
Add egg yolk and vanilla.

Blend in flour ¼ cup at a time.
Stir in crushed candy by hand.
In a separate bowl, beat the white of the egg until frothy.
Roll dough into 1 inch balls.
Dip top of each ball into egg white and then into sugar. Place on cookie sheet sugar side up.
Put thumbprint in top of each of each cookie and then top it with a chocolate kiss.
Bake 10 to 12 minutes.
Yields about 5 dozen cookies.

Contest Cookie Entry by Janie Pendleton

Christmas Butter-Cream Spritz Cookies

1 cup real unsalted butter, softened
1 (3 ounce) package cream cheese, softened
1 cup white sugar (can use Splenda)
1 egg yolk

1/2 teaspoon vanilla or almond extract
2 1/4- 2 1/2 cups all-purpose flour

Directions:

1. Preheat oven to 325 degrees F (165 degrees C).
2. Lightly grease cookie sheets.
3. In a large bowl, cream together butter, cream cheese, and sugar until light and fluffy. Beat in egg yolk and vanilla.
4. Stir in enough flour to make dough firm enough to put through press and blend well. (add food coloring now, if desired)
5. Chill dough for 30 minutes.
6. Drop dough by the spoonful and roll in powdered sugar and press jam in centers if desired, or use a cookie press to place onto prepared cookie sheets. If using floral cookie press design, make an indentation in the center with a small thimble, fill with raspberry or strawberry preserves, or can even press candy into the center of each cookie.
6. Bake for 11-14 minutes in preheated oven. Cookies should be still be pale.
7. Sprinkle with colored sugar or Jello powder, or can fill with the jam.
8. Let cool on wire racks.
9. Store in sealed container for up to one week, or can be sealed and frozen for up to two months. Enjoy!

If you would like to SUBMIT a recipe for future books, or be the first to know the next book I'm writing, PLEASE follow me on Facebook using the link below, to receive automatic updates on all CONTESTS, book GIVEAWAYS and book releases.

www.facebook.com/SamanthaBayarr

Available on KINDLE, NOOK and PAPERBACK

Available on KINDLE, NOOK and PAPERBACK

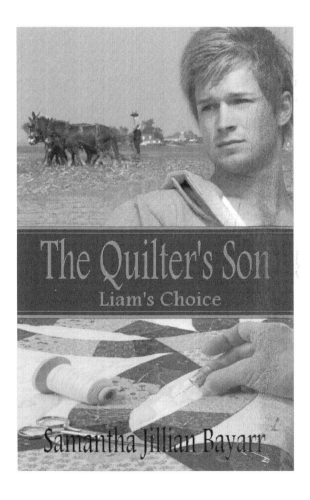

Available January, 2013

Made in the USA
Lexington, KY
06 February 2013